Whimsyland

Be Cre8ive with Lizzie B

BY LIZ & BETH HAWKINS

OF *LizzieB cre8ive!*®

Whimsyland
Be Cre8ive with Lizzie B

By Liz & Beth Hawkins of Lizzie B Cre8ive
Editor: Kent Richards
Technical Editor: Christina DeArmond
Book Design: Amy Robertson
Photography: Aaron T. Leimkuehler
Illustration: Lon Eric Craven
Production Assistance: Jo Ann Groves

Lizzie B Cre8ive
Website www.lizziebcre8ive.com
Retail shop www.shoplizzieb.com
Email lizziebgirls@gmail.com

Michael Miller Fabrics kindly provided the
fabric for the Topsy-Turvy project, which was
also a resource for selected design elements
in the book.

Published by:
Kansas City Star Books
1729 Grand Blvd.
Kansas City, Missouri, USA 64108

First edition, first printing
978-1-935362-07-4

Printed in the United States of America
by Walsworth Publishing Co., Marceline, MO
To order copies, call StarInfo at
(816) 234-4636 and say "Books."

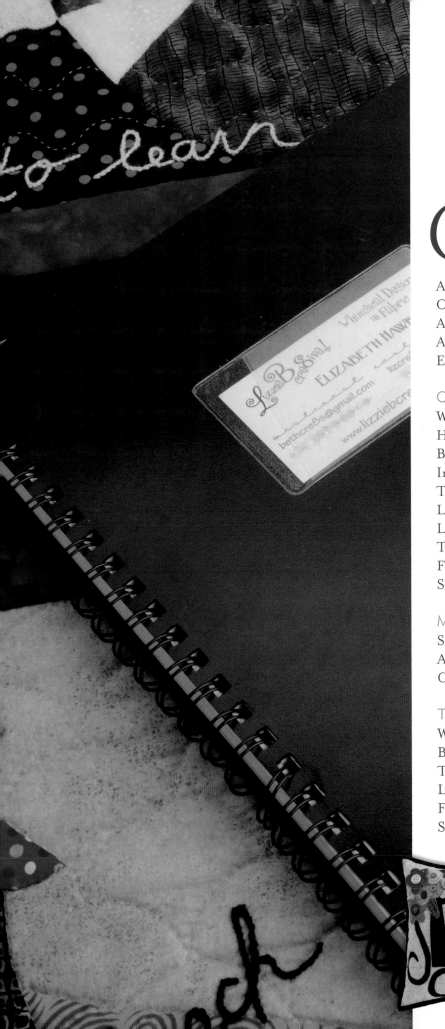

Contents

Who are these Lizzie B girls?

Elizabeth Hawkins (Liz) resides in Berwyn, Pennsylvania, with her husband, four children and Schnoodle. Her background is in fine arts and watercolor. She enjoys the conception and design side of Lizzie B and travels everywhere with the tools of her trade: a sketchbook and iPhone! She just never knows when she may need to snap a picture or do a quick sketch of an idea that pops into her head. When she's NOT busy sketching, stitching or playing taxi mom; she may be singing with The Noteables, playing her flute or pennywhistle, playing Guitar Hero, catching up with friends on Facebook, or in some incredibly rare but wonderful instances…reading a good book.

Elizabeth Hawkins (Beth) resides in Tucson, Arizona, with her husband, four children and Goldendoodle. She has a background in design and business. She's the Lizzie B pattern writer and bookkeeper, which requires quite a bit of attention to fine detail in both areas! She also travels with her iPhone, since she and Liz are constantly zapping pictures of fabric and designs back and forth to each other when they can't be together. When she's NOT busy doing math, writing patterns, stitching or playing taxi mom; she may be writing to her son in Mexico, catching up with friends on Facebook, talking to Mama C, cleaning up after her puppy and reading or listening to a good book before bed (trying really hard not to fall asleep mid-sentence).

Our Whimsical World

f you lived in a whimsical world, what would it look like? This is the question we asked ourselves as we took our first tentative step down the colorful pathway to what would become the very first Lizzie B book. We looked around our studios, our homes, and our lives, and took notice of the things that put a smile on our faces or warmed our hearts. Then we threw these things together and created the perfect recipe.

Laughter ringing through the house, like a ray of sunshine on a cloudy day. The sound of a favorite tune to inspire a smile and perhaps a forgotten memory. A warm, colorful quilt to wrap up in and make a cold winter's night feel like summer. An unassuming dream opening up the unconscious mind to unleash a flood of creativity. A wonderful friendship reminding us of our reasons to live. The flowers that continue to bloom every spring; the trees that stand tall, leaves rippling in the wind; the vines that fight to grow that one incredible bloom; the sky above like an ever-changing palette... all the beauty of nature continually adding color to our world. And lastly, the warmth, love, and encouragement from our families empowering us to be who we are.

Add to these fine ingredients a jazzy songlist playing in the background to keep us working into the wee hours of the morning. A plate of the best ever homemade chocolate chip cookies to give us nourishment. The chocolate stash tucked away "just in case." Our comfy jammies and workspace filled with quirky quotes, knick-knacks and tools of the trade to help inspire creativity. A sampling of all the things we've loved about our quilts and designs. And voilà...! The whimsical world of Lizzie B. Like Alice diving into Wonderland, we invite you to skip along the colorful pages of our book, taking time to stop along the way and remember to laugh, be inspired, smile, love, live and dream. We hope you love our world as much as we do and that it inspires you to create a little corner of your own world that makes you smile. **Welcome to Whimsyland!**

Our Sweet World

Recipe for: FABULOUS CHOCO CHIP COOKIES

From the Kitchen of: LIZZIE B

1 CUP BUTTER, ROOM TEMP
1½ CUP PACKED BROWN SUGAR
2 LARGE EGGS
1 tsp. VANILLA (TRADER JOE'S BOURBON VANILLA IS A MUST!)
2½ CUPS FLOUR
1 tsp. BAKING SODA
½ tsp. SALT (I LIKE COARSE SEA SALT FOR THAT SALTY/SWEET FLAVOR)
2½ CUPS CHOCOLATE CHIPS

1. BEAT TOGETHER BUTTER & BROWN SUGAR. ADD EGGS & VANILLA
2. MIX DRY INGREDIENTS TOGETHER. ADD TO BUTTER MIXTURE ALONG WITH CHOCOLATE CHIPS.
3. DROP BY 2 TBLS. PORTIONS ONTO COOKIE SHEET.
4. BAKE AT 400° FOR 6 MINUTES. (THEY WILL NOT LOOK COOKED - TAKE 'EM OUT ANYWAY. IF YA WANT OOEY-GOOEY THAT'S WHAT YA GOTTA DO!)

Our Musical World

Both Lizzie B girls ALWAYS have music in the background for inspiration. Here's their Whimsyland Playlist (downloadable at iTunes—search "Whimsyland" in the iMix section):

Sisters — The Puppini Sisters
Give Him the Ooh-La-La — Blossom Dearie
La Vie En Rose — Sophie Milman
If I Spoke French — Julia Rich
Oops! — Louis Armstrong
Under a Blanket of Blue — Stacey Kent
Java Jive — The Puppini Sisters
When I Take My Sugar to Tea — Jenna Mammina
My Heart Stood Still — Chet Baker
Coffee, Chocolate & Men — Jen Rathbun
Too Darn Hot — Mel Tormé
Anything Goes — Ella Fitzgerald
Honeysuckle Rose — Jane Monheit
I Will Survive — The Puppini Sisters
Someone To Watch Over Me — Sting
Dream A Little Dream of Me — The Beautiful South
Isn't It Romantic? — Chet Baker
In the Still of the Night — Neville Brothers
I've Got My Love To Keep Me Warm — Ella Fitzgerald
Will You Remember Me? — Susannah McCorkle
Don't Fence Me In — Ella Fitzgerald
I'm Putting All My Eggs In One Basket — Stacey Kent
They All Laughed — Mel Tormé
It Don't Mean A Thing — The Puppini Sisters
That Whimsical Spell — Joe Zapata, Darrell Brown

From the Bottom of Our Hearts...

We think this is the most daunting page in the entire book! Where do we even start? We'd like to thank Godiva, Lindt, Hershey, Nestle...etc. The makers of Diet Coke. Apple, for keeping the techie side of our business alive. All the restaurants who provide sustenance and inspiration to the Lizzie B team wherever we might be. And Oprah. (Just in case this book makes her list...)

But seriously, there were actual people involved in putting this book together. We must thank Doug Weaver and Diane McLendon at Kansas City Star for seeing something in us that might be book-worthy. Our editor, Kent Richards, who guided us through the process and when we shared our wacky ideas, he didn't go screaming for the hills asking to be assigned elsewhere. We swapped laughs and music along the way and couldn't have asked for a better adviser. Photographer Aaron Leimkuehler, who not only took beautiful shots of our projects in the studio, but got sent unsuspectingly to our wonky world to take on-site shots and had to endure a whole day with us. Good times, good times. Eric Craven, graphicsman extraordinaire, who worked like crazy to get all our scans and sketches to make complete sense. Also Jo Ann Groves and Christina DeArmond, who worked behind the scenes and we may never even know the hours they spent trying to make sense of our world! Amy Robertson, our art director, whose book design skills we have trusted implicitly. She had us figured out from the start, and even if we knew how to book-design, Amy still would have captured the "Lizzie B look" better than us. It would have taken us years (or possibly never!) to accomplish what this fabulous team has in such a short time.

As for those in our little quilty world whom we need to thank, there are many. But first and foremost is Mama C (otherwise known as Carole Price), without whom we could not even exist. The fact that she is Beth's mom makes this a very true statement in more than one way! She has been such a support to us from the start and has been our angel quilter, gladly stitching anything we throw her way. She stitched not one, but TWO "Whimsyland" quilt tops, and many other projects in this book. We also need to thank John Koncurat (Liz's brother) who knew nothing about quilting, but on a whim came to support us at our first market and has been with us ever since. He also forced us to make our first bean bag chair instead of letting us play out on the lake like everyone else while on vacation. Who knew it would have made such a splash at market that fall, and be the catalyst to prompt our first book? John knew. Though he hasn't stitched a quilt for us yet, he keeps us IN stitches with his multiple personalities. We'd also like to mention all of our dear quilting friends; Christine Reyes (Liz's sister) who is our website designer and Illustrator genius; fellow designers Annie Smith and Gina Halladay, who inspire and encourage us and give us honest feedback when we bounce our quirky ideas around. Mark Lipinski for telling us to always be true to ourselves and for treating us like queens (the kind with crowns...!) when we were really just newbies. Lauri Drean, who reads our blog, became our friend on Facebook, and ended up being our long-arm quilter for "Whimsyland." We still have never even met in person, but know that when we do, it'll be like meeting an old friend—she totally "gets" us and "Lizzie B'd" that quilt better than even we imagined! And thanks to Michael Miller Fabrics for providing the fabrics for Topsy-Turvy.

If we were at the Grammy's right now, the red light would be flashing like mad, the music would start to swell, and we'd be soon escorted off the stage! But we'll be escorted right out of our own families if we don't take a moment to mention them. Our parents, Bob & Carole Price and Pierre & Sharon Koncurat, who raised two girls in homes filled with love, creativity and a positive environment. Our siblings, who love and support us. Our husbands, Duane & Doug (brothers and great friends), who both had the good sense to marry an Elizabeth Ann. They love us through thick and thin (and we're NOT just talking about the effects of childbirth and our addiction to chocolate...) and truly give us the wings to fly. They also gave us the most fabulous children in the world... Chris, Ben, Josh, Zack, Trevor, Sienna, Keegan, and Adele. To whom we'd just like to say—sorry for all the Hot Pocket dinners and mornings without milk! Your mommies love you more than words can say and hope that one day, we'll grow up to be just like you.

And to God...who gave us a handful of talents, and each other. — *Liz and Beth Hawkins*

Appliqué The Lizzie B Way!

*Now, we by no means claim to have invented this technique…it is just one that is sometimes overlooked because it does require a little prep work before you get to stitch. But if traditional needleturn appliqué stresses you out, or just isn't fun, or doesn't look just the way you want it to… then **please**, give this a try. Because once you get the hang of this (and we promise it won't take long), your needleturn-agita will go away, and you will just want to appliqué everything in sight!*

HERE WE GO!

1. Reverse the pattern pieces when tracing onto freezer paper. We draw a **solid** line when tracing to indicate that we must turn and stitch, and a **dotted** line to indicate where we don't need to turn and stitch (because that part of the pattern will lie underneath another pattern piece). Just our little code, so we know what to do later. Don't forget to number your pattern pieces!

2. Double up! Before you cut out your patterns…**double** the freezer paper layer to make it a little heavier. Use a regular iron to adhere the layers together…(keep the pattern side up so you can still see your cutting lines, and make sure there is still one dull side and one shiny side).

3. Cut out your pattern pieces, right on the solid lines. And just to the outside of the dotted lines, so you can tell where they are. The smoother you cut, the smoother your fabric will look when appliquéd…so take your time around all the curves.

4. Press the shiny side of your patterns to the **wrong** side of the fabric.

5. Cut the fabric around the patterns, leaving a scant ¼" of fabric on all sides. Clip **all** inside curves just halfway to the paper pattern, and clip inside V's almost to the paper pattern.

SUPPLIES NEEDED FOR APPLIQUÉ:

- Freezer Paper
- Fabric Sizing or Starch (aerosol or liquid)
- Fabric Glue
- Small craft iron
- Small paintbrush
- Straw appliqué needles
- Silk or cotton thread
- Lightbox (optional…but makes pattern tracing so much easier!)
- Lapboard ironing surface (You really will want to use one…because the best part about this appliqué technique is that you can do it in your jammies on the sofa while watching a chick flick!)

6. Heat up your small iron, and get your starch ready. Spray a small amount of starch into a small dish (if you are using an aerosol, the starch will liquefy)…now you can "paint" it onto your fabric edges without spraying your entire ironing board or comfy chair!

7. Moisten just the edges of the fabric pattern piece. Use your iron to press the edges around and over the paper pattern (and because it is double-thick, this is much easier). Press until the starch dries and the edge is laying flat.

8. For outside curves, use the side of your small iron and curve around the paper pattern, pressing the fabric carefully as you go. It will pleat as you press, just make sure the pleats are on the back only and not to the outside edge. You will get better at this…and will be able to make entire curves that are completely smooth! **If** you press a point or pleat in there that you don't want, moisten it a little more, and try again. Much easier than ripping out appliqué stitches later that you are not happy about!

9. For inside curves, again, use the side of your iron and press the fabric right up to the paper edge. You will be pressing the bias out of the fabric as you go, which gives you a nice flat, smooth curve. Treat inner points just like you would an inner curve… press the fabric in there as much as you can, and you can stitch it perfectly later.

10. For outer points, just don't worry right now about all that "sticking-out" fabric. After all, we can do a little needleturn when we stitch! Press the point first in one direction, then the other, and worry about the rest of the fabric later. You will definitely burn your fingers if you try to get it all tucked in with the iron, **trust** us.

11. All those dotted line areas…just ignore them! They will be tucked under other pieces.

12. Carefully remove the paper pattern. You can use your iron to then press the piece one more time to make sure those edges stay down.

13. Place the paper pattern layout on a lightbox, and layer the appliqué shapes from back to front. (If your pattern uses a numbering system, then start with #1 and go from there.) You can glue the entire appliqué motif together, **before** placing it on the background block fabric! Glue the reverse of each piece **sparingly**, on the seam allowance. We like to use fabric glue that has a small applicator tip that allows a tiny dot of glue to be applied **just** where you want it. Glue just a few dots here and there...well below where you are going to stitch. For points, do not glue right **at** the point...leave it free so you can tuck in the excess fabric when you stitch.

14. Once the appliqué shapes are glued together, carefully transfer the whole thing to the background fabric, placing it just where the pattern instructions indicate. Glue down the outside edges of the motif.

15. So, now your **whole** appliqué block is turned, and secured in place. No pins to catch your thread on...no chalk marks to erase...no pattern pieces to remove later. And no extra stitching underneath the shapes...just stitch all the outer edges, and be sure not to miss any! We like to use silk thread in a matching color (neutrals or black work almost all of the time), but any good cotton appliqué thread will do.

Voilá! Now wasn't that easy?

Embroidery stitches

STEM STITCH

Working from left to right, bring the needle up through fabric on the line to be stitched. Take short, uniform stitches along the traced line, while holding the loop of thread towards the left side. Bring the needle up and out of the fabric to the left at the end of each previous stitch. Keep the stitches small and uniform.

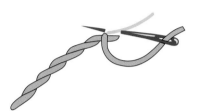

When stitching a curved line, make sure that the needle always passes the previous stitch on the inner edge of the curve. So, as a curve changes directions, you will need to "flip" your stitches too, in order to keep the stitches on the inner edges of the curves. Take smaller stitches if the curve is tight... this will create smooth curves!

BACK STITCH

Working from right to left, bring the needle up through fabric on the line to be stitched, starting on the LEFT side of the first stitch. Take short, uniform stitches along the traced line. Bring the needle up through the fabric at twice the length of a stitch. Place the needle back down on the right side, and repeat. Keep the stitches small and uniform. When stitching a curved line, take smaller stitches to create smoother curves.

begin

"Whimsyland" quilt, 66" x 88." Stitched by Carole Price and machine-quilted by Lauri Drean.

Whimsyland

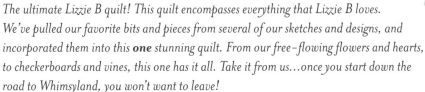

66" x 88"

The ultimate Lizzie B quilt! This quilt encompasses everything that Lizzie B loves. We've pulled our favorite bits and pieces from several of our sketches and designs, and incorporated them into this **one** stunning quilt. From our free-flowing flowers and hearts, to checkerboards and vines, this one has it all. Take it from us…once you start down the road to Whimsyland, you won't want to leave!

CUTTING INSTRUCTIONS

Cutting instructions are found under each block heading.

Before beginning the project, skip to the following headings and cut these larger pieces first so that you have enough fabric:

❀ **Borders** and **Scallops**, use 4 of the creams that measure ¾ yard for the outer borders.

❀ **Love block**, cut the background from one of the cream fabrics.

❀ **Smile block**, cut the background from one of the cream fabrics.

❀ Use the fat quarters to cut the backgrounds for the **Sunny**, **Live**, and **Cupcake blocks**, and the frame for **Smile**.

MOSAIC BACKGROUND BLOCKS

❀ From assorted black fabrics, cut 36 squares 3".

❀ From assorted cream fabrics, cut 90 squares 3".

1. Make four 9-patch blocks from the black fabrics, and ten 9-patch blocks from the cream fabrics, using the fabrics randomly in each block.

2. Cut each 9-patch block into four equal sections, as shown. The new blocks will measure 4". You should have 16 black blocks, and 40 cream blocks.

FABRIC REQUIREMENTS

- 9 different blacks, 1/2 yard each
- 8 creams, 3/4 yard each
- 6 tans, 1/4 yard each
- 5 greens, 1/4 yard each
- Fat quarters of: blue for Sunny block, dark purple for Smile frame, purple for Live block, and tan for Cupcake block.
- Assorted pieces (1/4 yard each) in the following colors: dark blue, yellow, dark yellow, 2 oranges, 3 turquoise blues, 4 purples, 4 pinks, 5 reds.
- Black for binding, 3/4 yard
- Perle Cotton, size 5, for embroidery, in black, dark red, purple, yellow, green, blue, pink-orange.
- 3 buttons for flower centers
- 1 small black button for doorknob
- 1/2 yard ribbon for bouquet
- Small glass beads for cupcake sprinkles

Templates on pages 56-80

3. Sew the 4" black blocks into rows of 4 blocks each, turning them in random directions and not worrying about fabric placement. It's okay if the same fabrics touch each other! Match seams where needed. Make 4 rows.

4. Sew the 4 black rows together to make a square that measures 14½". This completed background will be used for the Hearts block.

5. Sew the 4" cream blocks into rows of 4 blocks each, turning them in random directions. Make 10 rows.

6. Sew 5 cream rows together to make a block that measures 14½" x 18". Repeat to make two blocks.

7. Trim one of the cream blocks to measure 14½" x 16½". This completed background will be used for the Fleurs block.

8. Trim the remaining cream block to measure 12½" x 16½". This completed background will be used for the Flowerpots block.

CHECKERBOARD SECTIONS

See diagram on page 56.

1. For Checkerboards A and B, cut 12 tan 2½" squares, and 12 cream 2½" squares. Assemble as shown. Make 2 sections, and label as A and B.

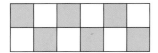

2. For Checkerboard C, cut 6 tan 2½" squares, and 6 black 2½" squares. Assemble as shown and label as C.

3. For Checkerboards D, E, and F, cut 12 tan 2½" squares, and 13 black 2½" squares. Assemble and label each section as shown.

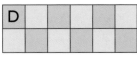

QUARTER-SQUARE SECTIONS

✿ From a black fabric and a cream fabric, cut two 7¼" squares of each.

✿ From a tan fabric, cut four 7¼" squares.

1. Cut each square on the diagonal twice, to make 8 black and 8 cream triangles, and 16 tan triangles.

2. Sew a black triangle to a tan triangle, with the black triangle on **top**, exactly as shown. Be careful to not stretch the bias edge as you sew. Press towards the tan triangle. Make 7 units.

tan/black

3. Sew a tan triangle to a cream triangle, with the cream triangle on **top**, exactly as shown. Press towards the tan triangle. Make 7 units.

tan/cream

4. Sew the triangle units together to form a 6.5" square, as shown. Make 7 squares.

5. Sew a vertical row of 4 squares together, and label as section H. Sew another vertical row with the remaining 3 squares and label as section G.

SHAPES BLOCK

❀ From a black fabric, cut a background 10½" x 4½".

❀ From a tan fabric, cut 2 strips 2½" x 4½", and 2 strips 2½" x 14½".

1. Sew the small strips to the sides of the background block, then sew the long strips to the top and bottom of the block.

2. Appliqué the shapes to the center of the block.

HEARTS BLOCK

❀ From a cream fabric, cut a right-side border 6½" x 14½".

❀ From another cream fabric, cut a bottom border 6½" x 20½".

❀ Use the black mosaic background square for the center of the block.

1. Stitch the right border to the side of the black mosaic background square.

2. Attach the bottom border to the unit.

3. Appliqué the two hearts in the center of the mosaic block. The scrolls and leaves will be appliquéd to the border blocks after the outer borders are sewn to the quilt center.

BIRDIE BLOCK

❀ Cut a black background 4½" x 8½".

❀ Cut 8 red 2⅞" squares and 8 cream 2⅞" squares.

1. Make the half-square triangles by placing a red and a cream square right sides together, lining up the corners. Draw a line from corner-to-corner. Stitch on each side of the line, a scant ¼" away. See diagram. Cut on the drawn line to make two units. Press open. Make 16 units.

LOVE BLOCK

❀ From a cream fabric, cut a background 14½" x 12½".

1. Appliqué the frame and the lettering shapes onto the center of the block.

2. Embroider the remaining lettering.

2. Sew a row of 6 half-square triangle squares together as shown. Make 2 rows.

3. Sew 2 squares together as shown. Make 2 units.

4. Assemble the block as shown in the diagram.

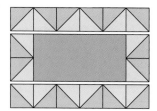

5. Appliqué the bird and leaves to the center and embroider the vine and the bird's eye.

VASE BLOCK

❁ From a cream fabric, cut a background 8½" x 12½".

❁ From a black fabric, cut a background 8½" x 4½".

1. Sew the backgrounds together, with the black fabric on the bottom.

2. Appliqué the vase to the center of the pieced background.

CINNAFLEUR BLOCKS

❁ From a black fabric, cut 2 rectangles 4½" x 12½" and one rectangle 6½" x 24½".

1. On the small blocks, appliqué the vine and single flower to the center of the block. Extend the vines to the raw edges of the block so they will get sewn into the seam when assembled. Make 2 identical blocks.

2. On the long block, appliqué the vine and trio of flowers to the center of the block. Extend the vines to the raw edges of this block also.

SUNNY FLOWER BLOCK

❁ From a blue fabric, cut a background 12½" x 10½".

1. Appliqué the flower to the center of the block. Extend the raw edges of the leaves into the seam allowance in the bottom corner of the block.

2. Embroider the smile using a stem stitch in black. Add small black buttons for the eyes.

SWEETHEART FLOWER BLOCK

❁ From a black fabric, cut a background 8½" x 10½".

❁ From a cream fabric, cut 2 strips 2½" x 8½" and 2 strips 2½" x 10½".

❁ From a tan fabric, cut 4 squares 2½".

1. Sew the 10½" strips to the sides of the black background.

2. Sew a tan square to each end of the 8½" strips, and then sew to the top and bottom of the background.

3. Appliqué the Sweetheart flower to the center of the block.

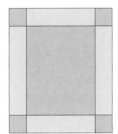

FLEURS BLOCK

✿ From a cream fabric, cut one top border 4½" x 12½", one bottom border 4½" x 22½", and two side borders 4½" x 16½".

✿ Use the tan mosaic background that measures 14½" x 16½" for the center of the block.

1. Pin the black frame pieces to the four border strips, matching the raw edges of the frames with the raw edges of the borders. Make sure the corners will match when assembled. Appliqué.

2. Sew the side borders to the mosaic block and then add the bottom border. The top border will be sewn when the entire quilt is assembled.

3. Appliqué the flowers to the center of the block. Tie a small bow from ribbon and tack to the center of the stems.

SMILE BLOCK

✿ From a cream fabric, cut a background 20½" x 16½".

1. Appliqué the frame to the center of the block, and then appliqué the lettering shapes in place.

2. Embroider the remainder of the lettering using a stem stitch.

HOURGLASS PIECED BLOCK

✿ From a tan fabric, cut 4 rectangles 2½" x 4½" (A), 8 squares 2½" (B), and 8 squares 2⅞" (C).

✿ From purple fabric, cut 4 squares 2⅞" (D).

✿ From black fabric, cut 4 squares 2⅞" (E).

✿ From pink fabric, cut 2 squares 2½" (F), and from orange fabric, cut 2 squares 2½" (G).

1. Make the C/D tan/purple half-square triangles (using 4 of the tan squares and the 4 purple squares) as explained in the Birdie block. Make 8.

2. Make the C/E tan/black half-square triangles (using the other 4 tan squares and the 4 black squares) in the same way. Make 8.

3. Piece the corner units as shown. Make 4.

4. Piece the outer center units as shown. Make 4.

5. Piece the center as shown. Make 1.

F	G
G	F

6. Assemble the block as shown. It should measure 12½" square.

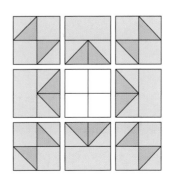

HOUSE BLOCK

❀ From a black fabric, cut a background 10½" x 16½".

❀ From assorted green fabrics, cut four 1" wide strips 6" long, and four 1¼" wide strips 6" long.

1. Sew the long sides of the green strips together randomly, varying the widths as you sew. Make a strippy piece of fabric that measures approximately 6" x 8", and press the seams all in one direction. Use this "new" fabric to cut the appliqué shape for the grass, lining up the arrows on the template with the strippy seam lines.

2. Appliqué the sky and house design to the center of the background block.

3. Embroider the window panes using a stem stitch, if desired, and add a small button for the doorknob.

FLOWERPOTS BLOCK

❀ Use the tan mosaic background that measures 12½" x 16½" for the center of the block.

1. Appliqué the flowerpots to the center of the block.

2. Add buttons to the centers of the flowers.

FUNKY FLEUR BLOCK

❀ From a black fabric, cut a background block 10½" x 8½".

1. Appliqué the flower to the center of the block.

2. Add a button to the center of the flower.

LIVE BLOCK

❀ From a purple fabric, cut a background rectangle 8½" x 20½".

❀ From a black fabric, cut one strip 2½" x 10½", one strip 2½" x 20½", and a square 2⅞".

❀ From a cream fabric, cut one strip 2½" x 10½", one strip 2½" x 20½", and a square 2⅞".

1. Use the black and cream squares to make two half-square triangles using the method explained in the Birdie block.

2. Sew the black 20½" strip to the right side of the background. Sew the cream 20½" strip to the left side of the background.

3. Sew one triangle unit to the right side of the cream 10½" strip, as shown. Sew to the top of the background. Sew the other triangle unit to the left side of the black 10½" strip, and sew to the bottom of the background.

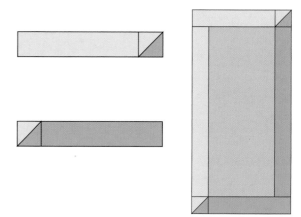

4. Appliqué the letter shapes and embroider the remaining lettering using a stem stitch.

PIECED HEART BLOCK

❀ From a cream fabric, cut a rectangle 4½" x 8½", 4 squares 2½", and 6 squares 2⅞".

❀ From an orange fabric, cut 6 squares 2⅞".

1. Use the 2⅞" cream and orange squares to make 12 half-square triangles using the method explained in the Birdie block.

2. Assemble the block as shown, placing the 2½" squares in the corners.

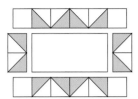

3. Appliqué the heart in the center of the block.

CUPCAKE BLOCK

✿ From a tan fabric, cut a background 10½" x 12½".

1. Appliqué the cupcake design to the center of the block.

2. Stitch small beads on the cupcake as "sprinkles."

DREAM BLOCK

✿ From a black fabric, cut a background 18½" x 6½".

✿ From a cream fabric, cut a top border 18½" x 6½".

✿ From another cream fabric, cut a side border 6½" x 12½".

1. Sew the top border to the background block, and then attach the side border.

2. Appliqué the letter shapes to the center of the block, and embroider the remaining lettering using a stem stitch. The scrolls and heart will be appliquéd to the border blocks after the outer borders are sewn to the quilt center.

Whimsyland continued

ASSEMBLE THE QUILT CENTER

1. Sew Love to the top of Shapes, and then to the right side of Hearts.

2. Sew Birdie to the top of Checkerboard A, then add a small Cinnafleur block to the bottom of Checkerboard A, and then sew the top frame border of the Fleurs block to the bottom. Sew to the right side of the previous unit.

3. Sew Checkerboard B to the top of Sunny Flower, then add the Sweetheart block to the right side. Add the Cinnafleur Trio block to the top. Sew to the left side of Fleurs.

4. Sew Checkerboard C to the right side of the Quarter-Square H section, then sew to the bottom of the Vase block.

5. Combine those large sections to complete the top half of the quilt, as shown.

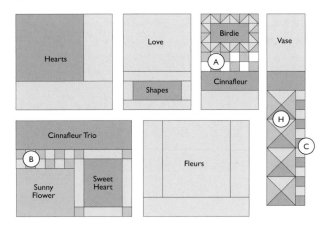

6. Sew Checkerboard E to the bottom of Quarter-Square section G, then add Checkerboard F to the left side.

7. Sew Checkerboard D to the bottom of Flowerpots, then sew to the right side of the previous unit. Add Smile to the top.

8. Sew the remaining small Cinnafleur block to the bottom of Hourglass, and then sew House to the right side.

9. Sew Funky Fleur to the left side of Pieced Heart, then sew to the bottom of the House unit.

10. Sew Live to the right side of the entire House unit.

11. Sew Cupcake to the left side of Dream, and then sew to the bottom of the House unit.

12. Combine those large sections to complete the bottom half of the quilt.

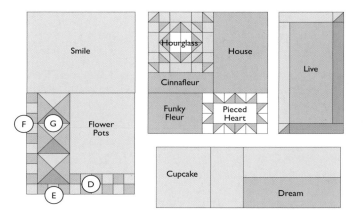

13. Sew the top and bottom sections of the quilt together to complete the quilt center.

Instructions continue on page 24.

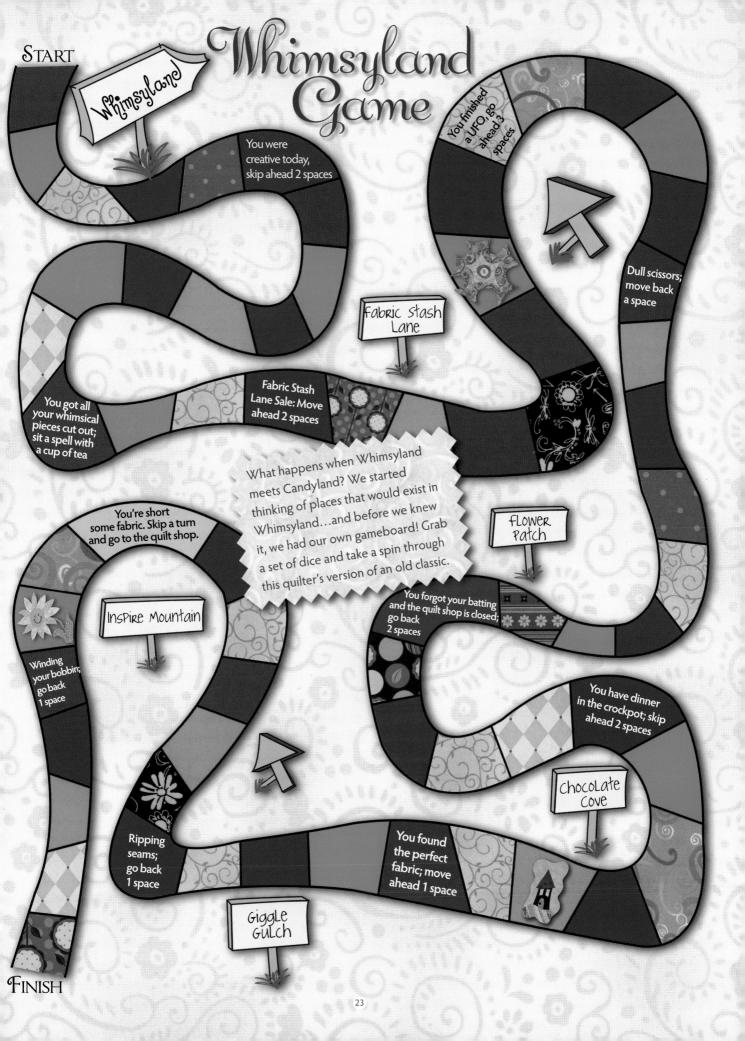

Whimsyland continued

BORDERS AND SCALLOPS

✿ From four different cream fabrics, cut 2 strips 6½" wide x width of fabric from each.

1. Join two of the same border strips together to create a longer length for each of the four borders.

2. Trim 2 borders to a length of 76½" for the sides.

3. Trim the remaining 2 borders to a length of 66½" for the top and bottom.

✿ From scrappy black fabrics, cut 45 rectangles approximately 3" x 5" for the scallops, and 4 squares 2" for the corner circles.

1. Use the scallop template to prepare 45 scallops for appliqué. Make 23 solid scallops, and 22 scallops with a cut-out circle in the center. Use the circle template to make 4 circles to appliqué at the corners and ends.

2. For the right side border, measure exactly ¼" in from the top edge (to be sewn to the Vase block) and place the first solid scallop. Line up the bottom raw edge of the scallop with the raw edge of the border. Place a scallop every 4", alternating solid and cutout scallops, until there are 16 scallops on the right side border. Appliqué the scallops. Sew the border to the right side of the quilt, matching the places where the scallops join to the seam lines in the quilt.

3. For the left side border, measure exactly ¼" in from the bottom edge (to be sewn to the Checkerboard F section) and place a solid scallop. Continue until there are 14 scallops on the border. Appliqué the scallops, and then sew the border to the left side of the quilt.

4. For the top border, measure exactly 6¼" in from the right edge (to be sewn to the top of the Vase block) and place a solid scallop. Continue until there are 8 scallops along the top border. Appliqué the scallops, and then sew the border to the top of the quilt.

5. For the bottom border, measure exactly 6¼" in from the left edge, and place a solid scallop. Continue until there are 7 scallops on the border. Appliqué, and sew the border to the bottom of the quilt.

6. Appliqué the circles to the top and bottom borders - one at each end of the row of scallops.

FINISH THE APPLIQUÉ

1. Appliqué the scrolls and leaves around the Hearts block, using the photo for placement. Embroider the ends of the scrolls using a stem stitch.

2. Appliqué the scrolls and heart around the Dream block, and embroider the scroll ends and tip of the heart using a stem stitch.

It's done! Quilt and bind as desired.

Opposite: Mirror, mirror, on the wall, the Lizzie B girls take a moment to recall… the reflection shows a smilin' Liz and Beth as they muse over their journey into Whimsyland.

"Honeysuckle Roses," 12" x 16." Stitched and framed by Beth Hawkins.

Honeysuckle Roses

Approx. 12" x 16"

Make this sweet bitty project in just an afternoon! Wool scraps, buttons, bits of thread, and ribbon give this little flower bundle a three-dimensional look. Frame this cutie to adorn any wall of your home, or the home of a good friend!

MAKE THE BLOCK

1. Cut the flower shapes and centers, and appliqué with the size 5 Perle Cotton, using a back stitch.

2. Trace single lines for the stems using a white chalk pencil or marker, and stitch the stems with size 3 Perle Cotton, using a back stitch.

3. Block by pressing with a steam iron from the wrong side.

4. Add buttons to the flower centers, and tie a small bow from ribbon and tack to the center of the stems.

5. Frame!

SUPPLY LIST
- Black fabric or felted wool for background (we used raw silk, washed and dried), 15" x 18" piece
- Assorted colors of felted wool for flowers, five 6" squares
- Yellows/oranges of felted wool for centers, five 1 1/2" squares
- 5 buttons for flower centers
- Perle Cotton, size 5, in colors to match wool
- Perle Cotton, size 3, green for stems
- Ribbon for bow, 1/2 yard
- Frame with a 12" x 16" opening

Templates on pages 66-67

Sisters at Heart

Sharing the same name is just the beginning

Once upon a time, there lived two little girls named Elizabeth Ann. One grew up in California, the other in Pennsylvania. Family and friends always knew the one from California as Beth. The one from Pennsylvania sat on her daddy's lap one day at the ripe old age of five and told him she wanted a NEW name, because EVERYONE had HER name! But like a good dad, he told her about a Queen named Elizabeth...so she scampered off with dreams of becoming Queen one day. But in the meantime, she demanded that everyone call her Liz. At the time she didn't realize just how important it was to keep her name, because somewhere on the West Coast lived her twin.

The girls grew up, like little girls do, and eventually got married. Beth met Duane in college. Their roommates were dating each other and Beth says he "stalked her by pretending to be a jogger." (Which he has never been!) Their first date was on the ski slopes, which totally won Beth's heart (that and the peach-colored Pinto). Years later, Liz met Doug in her own home while on summer break from college. He was a friend of her big brother and the first one to say "yes" to her brother's crazy idea of riding a bicycle across the United States, from sea to shining sea. She thought he was as insane as her brother, but also a little cute. The guys made it across the states in 28 days in August. In September, Doug and Liz spent 3 consecutive nights talking into the wee hours... by the end of which, they were engaged. He'd won her heart with his adventurous spirit (not to mention his yellow Trek and biking pants!) Little did the girls know that in some crazy cosmic way, they would marry into the very same family! Thus not only sharing the same first and middle names...but last names, too. It would be years before they realized the similarities did not stop there. Unfortunately, their paths in life took them separate ways early on in their sisterhood. Beth and her family moved around the United States, while Liz and her husband, flew off to live and start their family in France (after figuring out rather early on that Queen of England was NOT in her cards!) While they lived apart, they kept in contact the best they could. The first thing they discovered they both had in common was creativity. They LOVED to create! They tore through just about every crafty project through the '90s. From potpourri wreaths and stenciled walls, to clothing made from sweatshirts and dried flower arrangements. Then, at just about the same time, they both discovered...quilting!

This page: Bald baby Liz Koncurat on left, sweet ringlet Beth Price on right. Opposite: Liz Hawkins on left, Beth Hawkins on right.

Quilting was love at first sight. Liz's mom nearly had a heart attack when she heard Liz had bought her first sewing machine (she'd been trying to get Liz to sew for years!) Beth was living in the Southern US and decided to rekindle her quilt making skills (her mom taught her to sew by patching together dress scraps from her childhood wardrobe), by hunting down quilt shops, and falling in love with fabrics. For Liz, still living in France, fabric shopping was a bit more of a challenge. Not only was fabric very expensive, but 100% cotton was hard to come by. And quilt shops were non-existent. She had to be very creative in her fabric hunt by searching through second hand stores, using old sheets and duvet covers for backings, and finding ways to incorporate raw silk and linen into her quilts. By happy chance, right before Liz's first quilting class, she went to see Beth. And they found themselves shopping in the fabric section of the local 24-hour Wal-Mart at 2 am! After all, the nearest quilt shop was one state over, and certainly not open at 2 am. What they didn't know at the time was that would just be the first of many late nights they would spend together.

Liz went back to France, American quilt fabric in tow, to start her first quilt class. An American woman who just happened to live down her street taught the class. The class was made up of women from all over the world. They were to do a sampler made up of traditional blocks and appliqué. The teacher told them at the start that they would learn to do all the piecing by hand "just like their grandmothers had learned." Liz promptly raised her hand to let the teacher know that her grandmother was NOT a quilter, in fact, she crocheted and knitted, so could Liz just use her machine to piece then? She was labeled a troublemaker from the start. Beth found a favorite quilt shop about 90 miles away from home that offered great classes. So with her friend in tow, she headed out for the big city with machine in hand and a big smile on her face. After all, living in a house full of men demanded that some girl time be found, and quilting, along with the long drive, was the perfect answer!

Eventually, Liz moved back to the United States, but still never lived near Beth. Luckily their hubbies actually liked one another,

*Above right: The all-important tools of the trade...spools of thread and **chocolate**!*
Opposite: Beth at work choosing just the right mix of color and fabric. (Notice the ever-present Lizzie B mug with straw in the background.)

By happy chance, right before Liz's first quilting class, she went to see Beth. And they found themselves shopping in the fabric section of the local 24-hour Wal-Mart at 2 am!

Top 10 Things
Liz and Beth have in common
besides quilting:

1. Their full names (even both hubbies' names start with "D"…)

2. In-laws

3. Brighton—favorite accessory store

4. Chocolate (Any kind, from anywhere, at any hour. They're not picky!)

5. Similar sense of style (In fact, they're often caught wearing the exact same thing, on the exact same day, even though they live on opposite ends of the country! This can be embarrassing when they DO happen to be together.)

6. Music — their iPods even look similar. And songs have been known to inspire entire quilt designs…

7. Freezers are filled with the same things (quick & easy dinners for those long spurts of designing and quilting…) and if they are together, they don't mind a quick trip for an ice cream dinner!

8. Each have a dog of the poodle mix variety, and four kids (Liz has two girls and two boys—Beth's are all boys)

9. Finish each other's thoughts—it's quite the freak show!

10. Almost the EXACT same signatures…even more of a freak show. The bank has still not caught on.

as brothers should, and didn't mind when Beth and Liz made suggestions like having the families meet up for vacation-time in a city halfway between their two homes. Which at the time, happened to be Louisville, Kentucky…not a bad state for quilters to meet in (sometimes hubbies can be a little clueless!) The gals just mapped out directions to about every quilt shop in the area, and sent the dads and kids off to an amusement park. Which was to become a recurring theme (or possibly scheme?) for the two Hawkins' families.

Then in 2006, Beth was living in Tucson, Arizona, while Liz, going full circle, ended up back in her hometown in Pennsylvania. One spring break, she found she did not need much persuasion to leave the freezing weather to go visit Beth in the warm sunshine. This time, they packed some provisions and scooted the hubbies and kids off in the camper for a few days, pointed towards Sedona and the Grand Canyon. By the time they came back (dirty and hungry), Lizzie B Cre8ive had been born! Logo created, business cards printed, and five quilt designs in the works. Getting the business launched legally and financially was a more lengthy process since it took some coaxing to explain why Elizabeth Ann Hawkins needed both a partnership AND a joint checking account.

Needless to say, they've been sharing more than just their name on their quilting journey. The Lizzie B world is one where whimsy meets artsy with just a touch of sophistication. Together, Liz and Beth have found their niche in the quilting world. They design with an eye towards the imaginative, and look for inspiration in the things that they love and find comfort in: jazz music, pajamas and umm, chocolate! Traditional is not their focus, though they like to add bits of it here and there. They both enjoy appliqué because they can take it with them wherever they go. They love to embellish by adding detail and texture with simple notions and embroidery.

They share much more than just a name, and their love of the quilty world truly allows them to be sisters at heart.

Above: "I have monkeys and I'm not afraid to use them!" — Sometimes a mom/quilter needs to display warnings in her work zone. Opposite: Liz at work at her light table sketching, sketching, sketching. (Notice the ever-present Lizzie B mug with straw in the background.)

Live to learn

Inspire

learn to live...

then teach others!

Be Inspired!

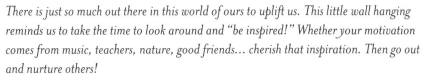

18" x 28"

There is just so much out there in this world of ours to uplift us. This little wall hanging reminds us to take the time to look around and "be inspired!" Whether your motivation comes from music, teachers, nature, good friends… cherish that inspiration. Then go out and nurture others!

MAKE THE BACKGROUND BLOCKS

❀ Mountains block: From cream fabric, cut a rectangle 10½" x 18½".

❀ Inspire block: From black fabric, cut a rectangle 5½" x 14½", and from brown fabric, cut 2 strips 2" x 18½" and 2 strips 2½" x 5½". Sew the small strips to the sides of the black rectangle, and the long strips to the top and bottom to complete the Inspire background.

❀ Schoolhouse block: From light blue fabric, cut a rectangle 10½" x 18½".

MAKE THE STRIPPY FABRICS

1. From 6 different blue fabrics, cut one strip 1" wide, one strip 1¼" wide, and one strip 1½" wide—each one 22" long. You will have 18 strips.

2. Sew the long sides of the blue strips together randomly, varying the fabrics and widths, until you have a piece of strippy fabric that is approximately 13" x 22". Cut the appliqué sections for the sky from this piece, lining up the arrows on the pattern template with the seam lines on the pieced fabric.

3. From 5 different cream fabrics, cut one strip 1" wide, one strip 1¼" wide, and one strip 1½" wide—each one 16" long. You will have 15 strips.

4. From black fabric, cut three 1" x 16" strips.

5. Sew the long sides of the cream and black strips together randomly, until you have a piece of strippy fabric that is approximately 12" x 16". Cut the appliqué sections for the hills from this piece, lining up the arrows on the pattern template with the seam lines on the pieced fabric.

FABRIC REQUIREMENTS

- Backgrounds: cream, light blue, black, and brown, one fat quarter of each
- Blues for sky, 6 fabrics, 1/8 yard each
- Creams for hills, 5 fabrics, 1/8 yard each
- Purples for mountains, 3 pieces 7" x 12" each
- Green for hill, 6" x 12" piece
- White for letters, 4" x 7" piece
- Assorted scraps of fabric and wool for remainder of appliqué

Wool:

- Ecru for mountains, 4" x 6" piece
- Black for music notes, 4" x 4" piece

Other Supplies:

- Binding, 1/3 yard
- Perle cotton, size 5, in white for lettering and other assorted colors to match wool.
- Assorted buttons for flower centers and schoolhouse bell and doorknob.

Templates on pages 81-87

Opposite: "Be Inspired!" quilt, 18" x 28," stitched and quilted by Carole Price.

Be Inspired! continued

APPLIQUÉ

✿ Cut out and appliqué the cotton shapes onto the blocks using your favorite appliqué method.

✿ Cut the wool pieces according to the pattern layouts, without adding an additional seam allowance.

✿ Stitch the pieces in numerical order. The wool is stitched with Perle Cotton, in matching colors, leaving the raw edges of the wool exposed, and using a back-stitch close to the edge of each shape.

EMBELLISHMENTS

✿ Embroider the lettering using a stem stitch, and Perle Cotton in size 5. Use the photo for placement of the lettering.

✿ Add assorted buttons to the flower centers as indicated in the photo, using matching Perle Cotton as thread. Stack two buttons together here and there for a dimensional look.

PUT IT ALL TOGETHER

✿ Sew the three blocks together vertically to finish the quilt.

Quilt, bind, and enjoy!

Opposite: The "Be Inspired!" quilt began with a rough drawing in Liz's always-handy sketchbook.

Live to learn

INSPI

lea

"DREAM" COMPANION

subject

date

Live to learn

INSPIRE

learn to live

then teach others!

"Inspire" sign, 8" x 18," stitched and quilted by Liz Hawkins.
A nice quick project to adorn any wall or give as a special gift.

Inspire Sign

8" x 18"

The "chalkboard" version of our "Be Inspired!" wall-hanging. A perfect addition to any creative room…be it a sewing studio, a music room, or a favorite teacher's classroom. Stitch it up in a jiffy, and whether you choose to frame it or quilt it, it's a quick and easy gift for any of your visionary friends!

CUTTING INSTRUCTIONS

❀ From black fabric, cut a rectangle 5½" x 14½".

❀ From brown fabric, cut 2 strips 2" x 18½" and 2 strips 2½" x 5½".

MAKE THE SIGN

1. Sew the small brown strips to the sides of the black rectangle, and the long strips to the top and bottom to complete the background.

2. Appliqué the lettering, apple, and flowers onto the block, using your favorite appliqué method. Use wool for some of the flowers, if desired, and stitch with Perle cotton in a matching color, using a back stitch. Stitch the remainder of the lettering with white Perle Cotton, size 5, using an outline stitch.

3. Press from the back side, and then add buttons to some of the flower centers.

4. The project is complete and ready for framing, if desired.

5. If you wish to quilt and bind your project, then layer with batting and backing, and quilt as desired.

6. Fold and press the ends of the casing strip over ¼", wrong sides together, and stitch down to secure. Fold and press the casing in half lengthwise, wrong sides together.

7. Pin the casing to the back of the quilted sign, centering along the top edge and matching raw edges. Baste in place.

8. Sew a quilt binding all around the edges of the quilted sign, catching the seam allowance of the casing as you stitch.

FABRIC REQUIREMENTS

- Black fabric for center, 1/4 yard
- Brown fabric for border, 1/6 yard
- White fabric for letters, 4" x 7" piece
- Assorted scraps of cotton and wool for apple, pencil, and flowers
- Perle cotton, size 5, in white for lettering, and other colors to match wool
- Buttons, if desired, for some flower centers
- Picture frame with 11" x 18" opening

For a quilted sign, assemble these materials:
- Backing fabric, fat quarter
- Batting 12" x 19" piece
- Binding, 1/4 yard
- Fabric for casing, one strip 2 1/2" x 16 1/2"
- Wood dowel, 1/4" diameter x 20" long
- Ribbon for hanger tie

Templates on pages 83-84

9. Handstitch down the folded edge of the casing to the back of the sign. Insert the dowel into the casing, and tie ribbon to the ends to form a hanger tie.

*The Lizzie Bean Bag Chair, very large,
stitched and quilted by Liz and Beth Hawkins.*

The Lizzie-Bean Bag Chair

What happens when a quilt fuses to a bean bag? Turns out, it's a cute and comfy chair that will brighten up any old room! The plush cover, blossoming with fuzzy, raw-edge appliquéd flowers, adds the coziness of a quilt to the comfort of this go-anywhere chair. You'll want to snuggle right in, grab a few of your favorite quilt mags, and stay awhile!

TEMPLATE INSTRUCTIONS

1. Use the diagram on page 88 as a guide to draw a beanbag **side panel template** on large paper, following the measurements for height and width.

2. Draw a circle on large paper that measures 32" across, and fold in half. Draw a line 1" from the folded straight edge, unfold the paper and cut along the drawn line. Use the larger side for the **bottom template**, and discard the smaller side.

3. Draw a circle that measures 10½" across for the **top template**.

CUTTING INSTRUCTIONS

❀ From the black fabric, cut 6 beanbag side panels, 2 half-circles for the bottom, and 2 small circles for the top.

❀ From the muslin fabric, cut 6 beanbag side panels, 2 half-circles for the bottom, and 2 small circles for the top.

❀ From the assorted flower fabrics, cut 10 B flowers, 9 C flowers, 6 D flowers, and 3 E flowers. From the yellow fabric, cut 10 A centers.

❀ From the green fabrics, cut 12 small leaves, 12 medium leaves, and 6 large leaves.

❀ From one blue-green vine fabric, cut 6 bias strips 1" wide x 18" long. From the other blue-green fabric, cut 6 bias strips 1½" wide x 18" long.

QUILTING INSTRUCTIONS

1. Layer the black pieces (6 beanbag side panels, 2 bottom half-circles, and only 1 top circle) with cotton batting and a muslin backing fabric, and quilt as desired.

FABRIC REQUIREMENTS
- Black background, 5 yards
- Muslin for inner beanbag and quilted backing, 10 yards
- Assorted reds/pinks/oranges for flowers total of about 1 3/4 yards
- Yellow for flower centers, one fat quarter
- 2 blue-greens for vines, fat quarter of each
- 3 greens for leaves, fat quarter of each
- Sew-on Velcro, 1" wide, 2 yards
- Cotton batting, Queen size, or batting scraps to equal 45" x 170"

Templates on pages 88-91

2. Trim the excess batting and backing away to match the raw edge of the beanbag panels.

RAW-EDGE APPLIQUÉ INSTRUCTIONS

1. On a black beanbag side panel, place a large flower E just a tad up from the center and pin in place. Tuck in two large leaves, one on the top and one on the bottom of the flower. *See figure 1 on page 43.*

2. Stitch around each of the leaves, about ¼" in from the raw edge, and then add a medium leaf to the top of each. Stitch around the medium leaves, and then add a small leaf to the top, and stitch.

3. Stitch around flower E, about ¼" in from the raw edge, making sure that the leaves are tucked underneath the stitching. Add flowers D, C and B, stitching around each layer. Add the yellow center A and stitch.

4. Repeat to make 3 panels with large flowers.

5. On another black beanbag side panel, place a flower C on the top half, towards one side. Place a flower D just below it, towards the other side. Pin both in place. *See figure 2 on page 43.*

6. Pin a 1½" bias strip and tuck it under the small flower, curving it towards the top edge. Trim it to match the raw edge of the top of the panel. Pin another 1½" bias strip under the medium flower, curving it towards the bottom raw edge, and trim. Stitch both strips ¼" away from each side. Layer the 1" strips right on top of the 1½" strips, and sew those in place.

7. Stitch around the small flower C shape, and add flower B and center A to complete.

8. Stitch around the medium flower D shape, and add flowers C and B, and center A to complete.

9. Add a leaf to both stems, layering and stitching a medium and small leaf to each.

10. Repeat to make 3 panels with small & medium flowers.

11. Pin the two black top circles (one quilted, and one not) right sides together, and stitch around the edge, leaving about a 3" opening. Clip curves, turn right side out, and press. Hand-stitch the opening closed.

12. Raw-edge appliqué a flower to the center of the circle, using flower B and center A.

SEWING INSTRUCTIONS
MAKE THE INNER BEAN BAG

1. Make the inner bean bag first, using the six muslin side panels. Sew the long sides of two panels, right sides together, using ½" seams. Continue sewing panels in the same manner, and then sew the first panel to the last, to create a large circle.

2. Turn and press under a ¼" seam allowance of the straight sides of the bottom half-circles.

3. Pin and sew a length of velcro across each straight edge, covering the raw edge that was pressed under.

4. Stick the velcro edges together, to form a complete circle. Stay-stitch the ends of the velcro all together, about ½" in, so that the two halves are joined.

5. Divide and mark the bottom circle into six equal sections, and pin the inner bean bag in place, right sides together. Ease the fabric so that it will fit, and sew around the entire circle, using a ½" seam allowance. Open up the velcro at the bottom, and turn right side out.

6. Pin the two top circles right sides together, and stitch around, leaving about a 3" opening. Clip curves and turn right side out, and press.

7. Flatten out the top opening of the bean bag liner, and cover the opening with the top circle. Carefully pin in place, and topstitch the circle onto the liner to complete the inner bean bag.

MAKE THE OUTER BEAN BAG

1. Make the outer bean bag by sewing the long sides of all six panels together, alternating the large flower panels with the small/medium flower panels, but do **not** yet join the last panel to the first panel.

2. Press open each seam and from the right side, topstitch a scant ¼" on each side of the seam.

3. Join the first and last panels, press the seams open, and topstitch.

4. On one bottom half-circle, press ¼" of the straight side towards the right side of the fabric. Stitch one side of a length of velcro along the edge, to the right side of the fabric.

5. On the other bottom half-circle, press ¼" of the straight side towards the wrong side of the fabric. Stitch the other length of velcro along the edge, to the wrong side of the fabric.

6. Stick the velcro edges together, to form a complete circle. Stay-stitch the ends of the velcro all together, about ½" in, so that the two halves are joined.

7. Divide and mark the bottom circle into six equal sections, and pin the bean bag in place, right sides together. Ease the fabric so that it will fit, and sew around the entire circle, using a ½" seam allowance. Open up the velcro at the bottom, and turn right side out. Press the seams open and topstitch all along the circular bottom edge.

8. Flatten out the top opening of the bean bag, and cover the opening with the finished top circle. Carefully pin in place, and topstitch the circle onto the bean bag twice, once close to the edge of the circle, and again about ¼" away from the first stitching.

FLUFFING AND STUFFING!

✿ After you have completed the outer bean bag, you may fluff the appliquéd flowers! The easiest way to do this is with a chenille brush, sold in quilt stores. Spritz a little water on the raw edges of the flowers and stems, a little back and forth with the brush…and the edges will fluff nicely. You may need to trim away some of the longer threads.

✿ Place the muslin lining inside the bean bag, with the velcro openings perpendicular to each other (like an "X"). Stuff the lining with "bean bag filler" and securely close the velcro. Close the velcro on the outer bean bag. Enjoy!

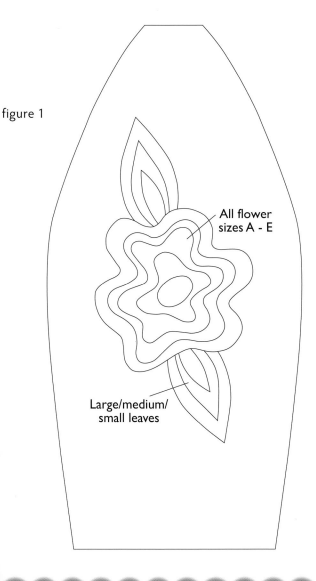

figure 1

All flower sizes A - E

Large/medium/ small leaves

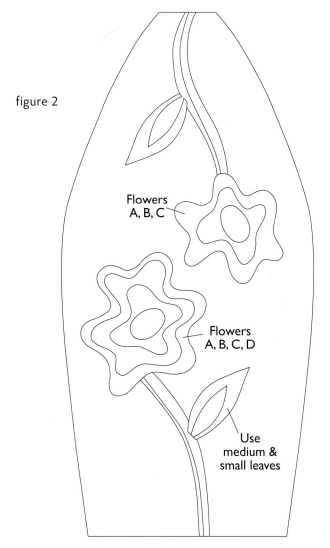

figure 2

Flowers A, B, C

Flowers A, B, C, D

Use medium & small leaves

A Rose By Any Other Name

It's a small, small world

Finding the right name is always a tough job. If you've ever had to name a child, you'll know what we're talking about! You have to find a first name that sounds pleasant, then you have to see if it still sounds good with the last name; and if it passes these two tests, the name goes into the final round. The "who-do-you-know-with-that-name" test. This one is a doozy because one person might associate a runny-nosed kid with one name, and another name may conjure up a bully, a smart-aleck or a nose-picker. And then you're back to square one!

So maybe it's not quite the same when finding a business name, but there are similarities, certainly. Maybe it doesn't have to sound good with a last name, but it does need to roll off the tongue nicely, and there definitely can NOT be any negative association connected to the name. After all, one doesn't want to doom one's business before it even gets off the ground! And so it was when we first sat down to mull over names for our new venture together. Having the same REAL name seemed like it would make finding a business name a cinch. Not so. Because how do you take that name and make it appealing? Interesting? Fun? Instead of consulting books and sites on names...we got out the laptop and conjured up trusty Google to help us in our search.

We wanted to find something that signified our matching names so we rambled off all the versions of Elizabeth we'd ever heard or been called: Liz, Lizzie, Izzy, Liza, Lizard, (and LizardBreath, courtesy of Beth's big brother!), Eliza, Beth, Betty, Betsy, Bessie, Bette...etc. The list went on and on! After much deliberation, we whittled it down to Lizzie B. The creative part was taken from a craft business that Liz had started years before on her own called "Everything Cre8ive." We loved how putting Lizzie B with the Cre8ive was not only a NAME but also a directive, so to speak, to "B Cre8ive"! Finally, we had a name! But would it pass the Google test? Were there other Lizzie B quilter's out there already in business? The first Google of Lizzie B brought up a site with a picture of a singer with her guitar. She lived in England, and since her name had nothing to do with quilting, we thought we were pretty safe there. Then Beth clicked on a song sample so we could hear this Lizzie B (had to make sure we could be associated, you know?)... and Liz could NOT believe her ears! She had heard Lizzie B before!

Just months earlier she'd been in London with her husband. It was a chilly January weekend and Doug's 40th Birthday. They were enjoying the city and traveling mostly by Tube to keep warm. One evening they were on their way to a show and decided to get off at the Piccadilly station and walk to the West End. As they were riding up one of the many, many escalators they heard a busker tucked away in the corner of the station, set up with a microphone and guitar and singing a familiar love song. *"Some say love...it is a river..."* she sang slowly in a low, sultry voice, but every time someone threw coins in her guitar case she'd stop mid-stanza and say *"thank you, thank you very much"*...sounding very Elvis-like. Then she'd jump right back where she left off. *"...that drowns, the tender reed...thank you, thank you very much..."* Doug and Liz chuckled over the performance a bit and went off on their merry way. But through the entire weekend, EVERY time they went in or out of Piccadilly, there she was! Singing the exact same song in the exact same tone...they suspected she never once even finished the song! *"Just remember, in the winter, far beneath the bitter snows...thank you, thank you very much..."* Guess what song boomed from the speakers when Beth clicked the "play" button on Lizzie B's site? *"...lies the seed, that with the sun's love, in the spring...becomes the rose"*!

What a small, small world we live in. We wondered for a few moments whether or not we should think of yet another name. Would people do a search for Lizzie B looking for quilts and be confused to find a singer? In the end, we thought not. And the coincidence of unknowingly stumbling upon the other Lizzie B was just too funny. We hope that somewhere out there, the guitar-playin' Lizzie B doesn't mind sharing her name with two Elizabeth Ann's. To Lizzie B, wherever she may be...*Thank you, thank you very much.*

> We wanted to find something that signified our matching names so we rambled off all the versions of Elizabeth we'd ever heard or been called: Liz, Lizzie, Izzy, Liza, Lizard, (and LizardBreath, courtesy of Beth's big brother!), Eliza, Beth, Betty, Betsy, Bessie, Bette...etc. The list went on and on!

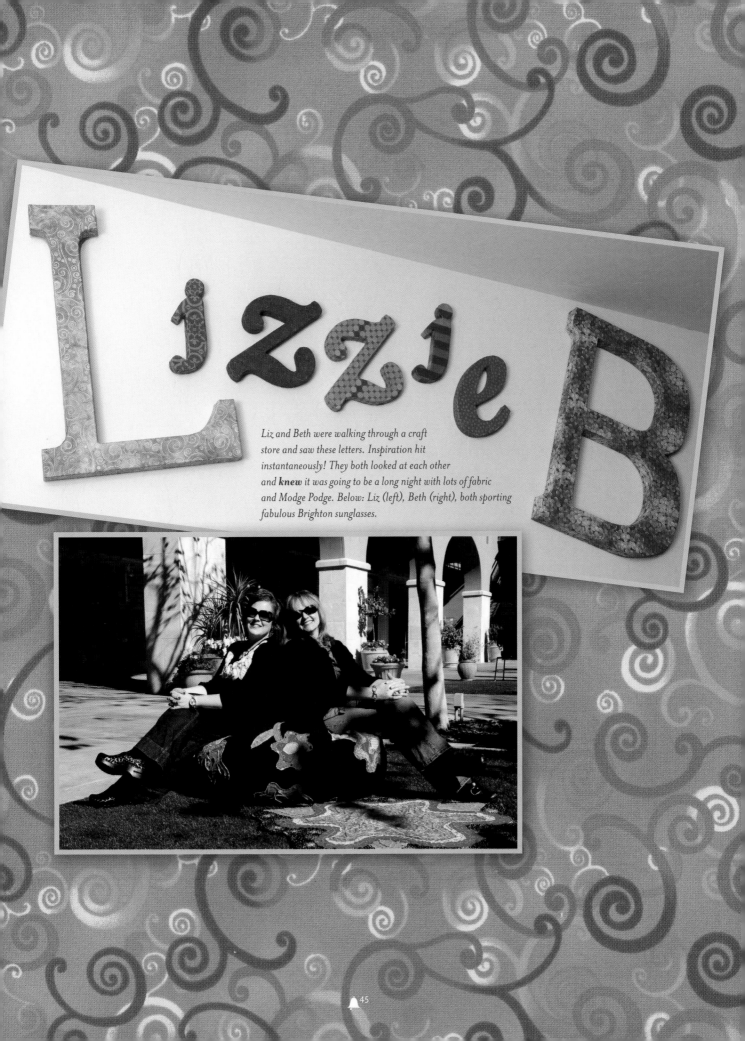

Lizzie B

Liz and Beth were walking through a craft store and saw these letters. Inspiration hit instantaneously! They both looked at each other and **knew** it was going to be a long night with lots of fabric and Modge Podge. Below: Liz (left), Beth (right), both sporting fabulous Brighton sunglasses.

A good laugh is sunshine in a house

LAUGH

Laugh

A Good Laugh
18" x 28"

There is just nothing better than the sound of laughter ringing throughout a house. The good ole belly-achin' kind that gets the tears streaming out of the corners of the eyes, that's what we're talking about! This quilt adds a bit of sunshine to your home and a reminder to **laugh** *each and every day. So go ahead...get your giggle on!*

MAKE THE BACKGROUND BLOCKS

❀ **Sunshine block:** From light blue fabric, cut a rectangle 9½" x 18½".

❀ **Houses block:** From another light blue fabric, cut a rectangle 8½" x 18½".

❀ **Laugh block:** From black fabric, cut a rectangle 5½" x 12½", and from cream fabric, cut 2 strips 3½" x 5½" and 2 strips 3½" x 18½".

❀ Sew the small strips to the sides of the black rectangle, and the long strips to the top and bottom to complete the Laugh background.

MAKE THE STRIPPY FABRICS

1. From 6 different blue fabrics, cut one strip 1" wide, one strip 1¼" wide, and one strip 1½" wide—each one 18" long. You will have 18 strips.

2. Sew the long sides of the blue strips together randomly, varying the fabrics and widths, until you have a piece of strippy fabric that is approximately 12" x 18". Cut the appliqué sections for the sky from this piece, lining up the arrows on the pattern template with the seam lines on the pieced fabric.

3. From 6 different green fabrics, cut one strip 1" wide, one strip 1¼" wide, and one strip 1½" wide—each one 18" long. You will have 18 strips.

4. Sew the long sides of the green strips together randomly, until you have a piece of strippy fabric that is approximately 12" x 18". Cut the appliqué sections for the hills from this piece, lining up the arrows on the pattern template with the seam lines on the pieced fabric.

FABRIC REQUIREMENTS

- Backgrounds: 2 light blues, 1 cream, and 1 black, fat quarter of each
- Blues for sky, 6 fabrics, 1/8 yard each
- Greens for hills, 6 fabrics, 1/8 yard each
- Green for letters, 1/6 yard
- Black for scrolls, 1/8 yard
- Yellow for sun, 8" x 8" piece
- Yellow for rays, 1/6 yard
- Blacks for house, 3 pieces 4" x 5" each
- 3 assorted fabrics for roofs, 4" x 5" each

Other Supplies:

- Assorted scraps of fabric and wool for remainder of appliqué
- Binding, 1/3 yard
- Perle cotton, size 5, in black for lettering and other assorted colors to match wool
- Assorted buttons for flower centers and doorknobs
Templates on pages 92-97

Opposite: "Laugh a Good Laugh" quilt, 18" x 28." Stitched and quilted by Carole Price.

Laugh A Good Laugh continued

APPLIQUÉ

✿ Cut out and appliqué the cotton shapes onto the blocks using your favorite appliqué method. Two of the rays of the sun will need to be appliquéd after the quilt is assembled.

✿ Cut the wool pieces according to the pattern layouts, without adding an additional seam allowance. Stitch the pieces in numerical order. The wool is stitched with Perle Cotton, in matching colors, leaving the raw edges of the wool exposed, and using a back-stitch close to the edge of each shape.

EMBELLISHMENTS

✿ Embroider the lettering using a stem stitch, and Perle Cotton in size 5. Add assorted buttons to some of the shapes in the sun, and some flower centers, using matching Perle Cotton as thread. Stack two buttons together here and there for a dimensional look. Add buttons to the doors of the houses.

PUT IT ALL TOGETHER

✿ Sew the three blocks together vertically to finish the quilt. Complete the appliqué on the sun. Quilt, bind, and enjoy!

Left: The quilt's sketchy beginnings. Opposite: The small quilt in the foreground along with the Lizzie B pincushions on the shelf add just another splash of color to Beth's mosaic cabinet, which she created years ago when her boys were younger. (They helped with the plate and pottery smashing!) Beth painted one of her favorite quotes onto an old window that she salvaged to use as the cabinet door.

A good laugh is sunshine in a house

LAUGH

"Laugh Pillow," 11" x 18." Stitched and quilted by Beth Hawkins.

Laugh Pillow

11" x 18"

The last laugh? Never! This is just another chuckling reminder to invite humor into your home. We made ours into a pillow, but it can also easily be framed or quilted like "Inspire!"

CUTTING INSTRUCTIONS

✿ From black fabric, cut a rectangle 5½" x 12½" for the pillow center, and 2 strips 2¼" wide x width of fabric for the pillow binding.

✿ From cream fabric, cut two strips 3½" x 5½" and two strips 3½" x 18½" for the border. Cut two rectangles 11½" x 21" for the backing.

MAKE THE BLOCK

1. Sew the small cream strips to the sides of the black rectangle, and then sew the long cream strips to the top and bottom, to complete the block.

2. Appliqué the lettering, scrolls, and flowers onto the block, using your favorite appliqué method. Use wool for some of the flowers, if desired, and stitch with Perle cotton in a matching color, using a back stitch. Add buttons to some of the flower centers.

3. Layer the block with batting and a muslin backing and quilt as desired.

MAKE THE PILLOW

1. Press the backing rectangles in half, wrong sides together, so that they measure 11½" x 10½".

2. Place one of the rectangles on the wrong side of the quilted pillow front, matching raw edges towards one side. The fold of the backing fabric will be towards the center. Pin along the raw edges.

FABRIC REQUIREMENTS
- Black fabric for center and binding, 1/3 yard
- Cream fabric for front and back, 5/8 yard
- Black fabric for scrolls, one fat quarter
- Green fabric for letters, 1/6 yard
- Muslin for pillow top backing, 12" x 19"

Other Supplies:
- Assorted scraps of cotton and wool for flowers
- Perle cotton, size 5, in colors to match wool
- Buttons, if desired, for some flower centers
- Batting for pillow top, 12" x 19"
- Pillow form, 11" x 18"

Templates on pages 96-97

3. Place the other rectangle on the wrong side of the pillow front, towards the **other** side, so that the folded edge is also near the center and is overlapping the first backing rectangle. Pin.

4. Baste along the raw edges, around the entire pillow rectangle.

5. Stitch the ends of the two black binding strips together to create a longer length. Fold in half lengthwise, wrong sides together, and sew the raw edge of the binding to the front of the pillow, ¼" from the raw edges, and through all layers of the pillow and backing. Pivot at the corners, just like sewing on a quilt binding. Handstitch down on the back side, and stuff with a pillow form to fit.

Topsy-Turvy Duvet Cover, 100" square, made from the "Andalucia" fabrics
from Michael Miller, and sewn together by Beth Hawkins.

Topsy-Turvy Duvet Cover

100" square…for a big ol' bed

A fun quilt…without quilting! Is the idea of making a King or Queen sized quilt for your bed just too enormous to contemplate? Here's the answer to a beautiful bedroom, with no stress! This project calls for many spectacular fabrics sewn together in a "topsy-turvy" kind of way. But instead of quilting, we turned this enormous "quilt" into a duvet cover. Whip it up in a long afternoon, pop in a down comforter, and throw it on your bed…no quilting required! Be sure to cuddle up with a good book, while you admire your fabulous fabric choices and brilliant handiwork!

CUTTING INSTRUCTIONS

❖ Cut 4 rectangles of each fabric, and label:
Fabric A – 12" x 18"
Fabric B – 19" x 18"
Fabric C – 22" x 18"
Fabric D – 19" x 13"
Fabric G – 21" x 19"
Fabric H – 21" x 16"
Fabric I – 13" x 15"
Fabric J – 13" x 20"

❖ Cut 2 rectangles of each fabric, and label:
Fabric E – 19" x 22"
Fabric F – 19" x 22"

FABRIC REQUIREMENTS

Use 10 different fabrics for this project:
- 3 fabrics (A, E, F) – 3/4 yard each
- 3 fabrics (D, I, J) – 1 yard each
- 3 fabrics (B, H, G) – 1 1/4 yards each
- 1 fabric (C) – 1 1/3 yard
- One King-size flat sheet, or enough fabric pieced to make a 101" square for the back
- Snap-tape, 7/8" wide, 2 yards

SEWING INSTRUCTIONS

To piece the fabrics, all seam allowances are ½". After a seam is sewn, press the seam allowance to one side, and from the front, topstitch the layers down, ¼" from the seam.

1. Sew A to B to C as shown. Repeat to make 4 sections.

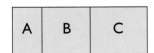

2. Sew D to E as shown. Make 2. Sew D to F as shown. Make 2.

3. Sew G to H as shown, and I to J as shown. Make 4 sections of each.

4. Sew all sections together to make one unit that measures 51" square. Make 4 units.

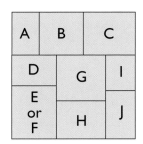

5. Sew all four sections together, rotating the blocks as shown in Figure 1. The whole duvet top should measure 101" square.

DUVET ASSEMBLY INSTRUCTIONS

1. Trim the sheet or fabric back for the duvet to 101" square.

2. Turn and press ¼" along one edge of the duvet back, right sides together. Repeat for one edge of the duvet top.

3. Along the pressed edge of the duvet back, measure 16" from the corner, and pin one side of the snap tape in place, right along the folded edge, to the **right** side of the duvet back. Leave the end of the snap tape raw (do not fold under) and stitch along all four sides of the snap tape, using a zipper foot if necessary. Repeat for the duvet top, again stitching to the **right** side, and make sure that the snaps will line up the same on both the back and the top.

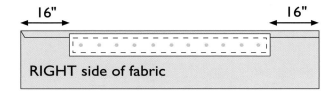

4. Pin the duvet top to the duvet bottom, right sides together. Stitch along the three remaining sides, using a ½" seam.

5. Stitch the open end of the bottom, from the corner to about ¼" over the end of snap tape, using a 1" seam. Trim away the excess seam allowance so the corner will turn inside out. Repeat for the other side.

Opposite: Shake a downy duvet into this colorful cover, toss it on the bed and add a bunch of fluffy pillows for the perfect whimsical touch.

6. Turn the entire duvet cover right side out, and press the seam edges flat. The snap tape will tuck under on the bottom edge and be "hidden" when fastened. Start at one end of the snap tape and topstitch about 1" from the edge.

7. Fill the duvet cover with a fluffy down comforter, toss it on your bed, and...sweet dreams!

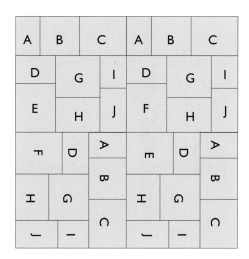

Figure 1

Whimsyland templates

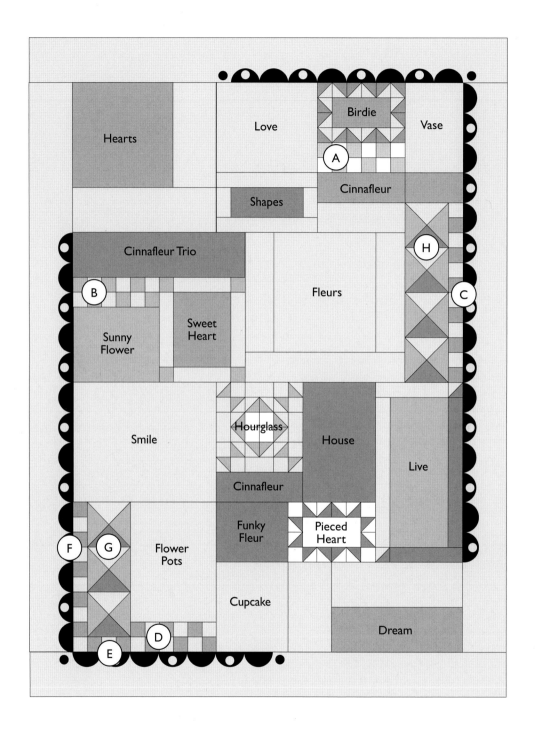

Hearts

Love

Birdie

Vase

A

Cinnafleur

Shapes

Cinnafleur Trio

H

B

C

Fleurs

Sunny
Flower

Sweet
Heart

Smile

Hourglass

House

Live

Cinnafleur

F

G

Funky
Fleur

Pieced
Heart

Flower
Pots

Cupcake

Dream

D

E

Whimsyland Hearts Block

Whimsyland Hearts Block

4

1

Make 4

2

3

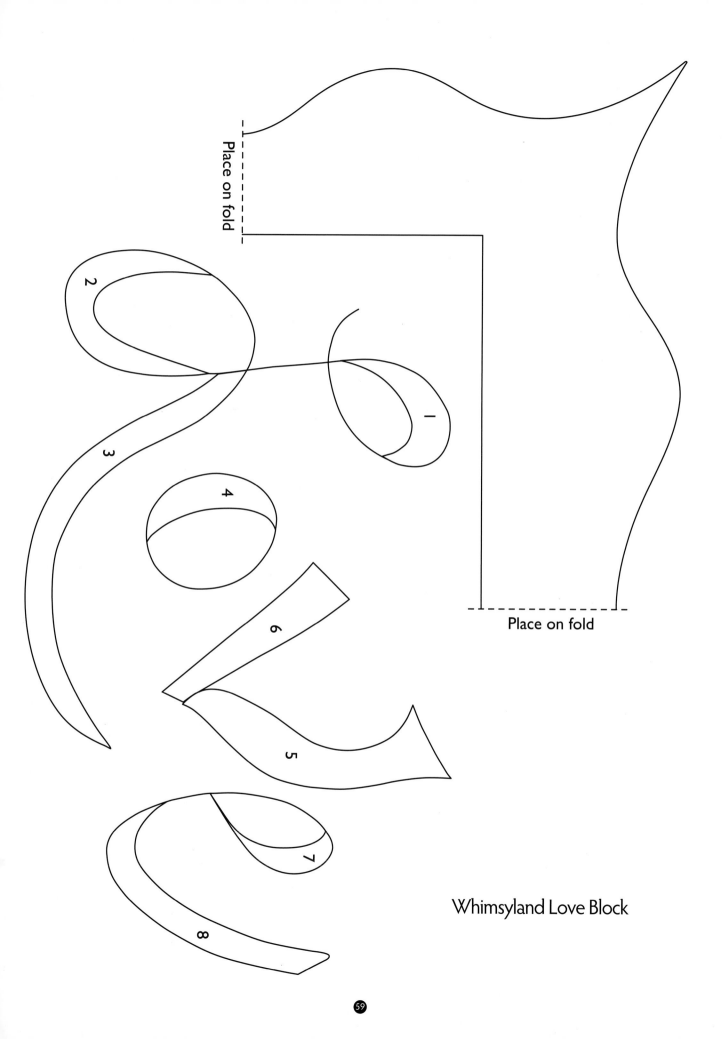

Place on fold

Place on fold

Whimsyland Love Block

Whimsyland Shapes Block

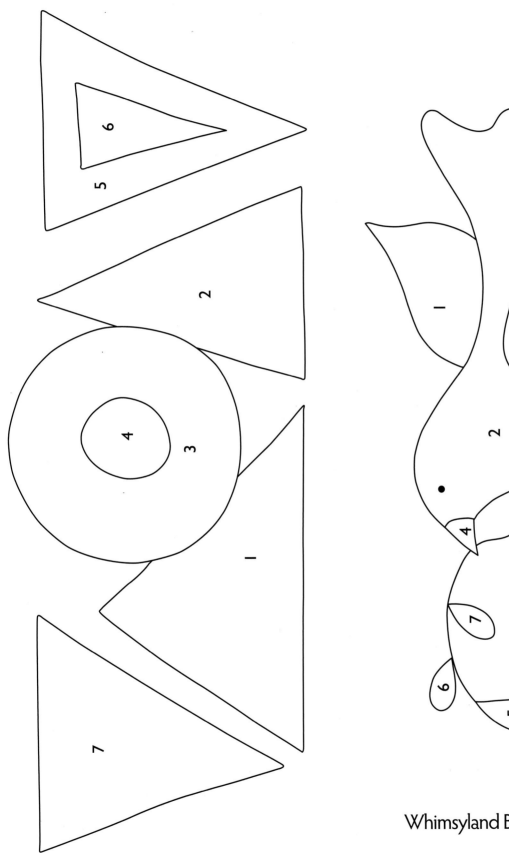

Whimsyland Birdie Block

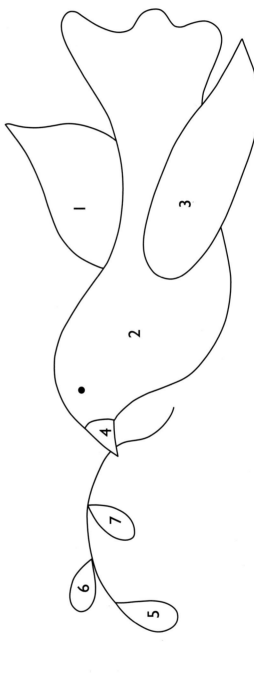

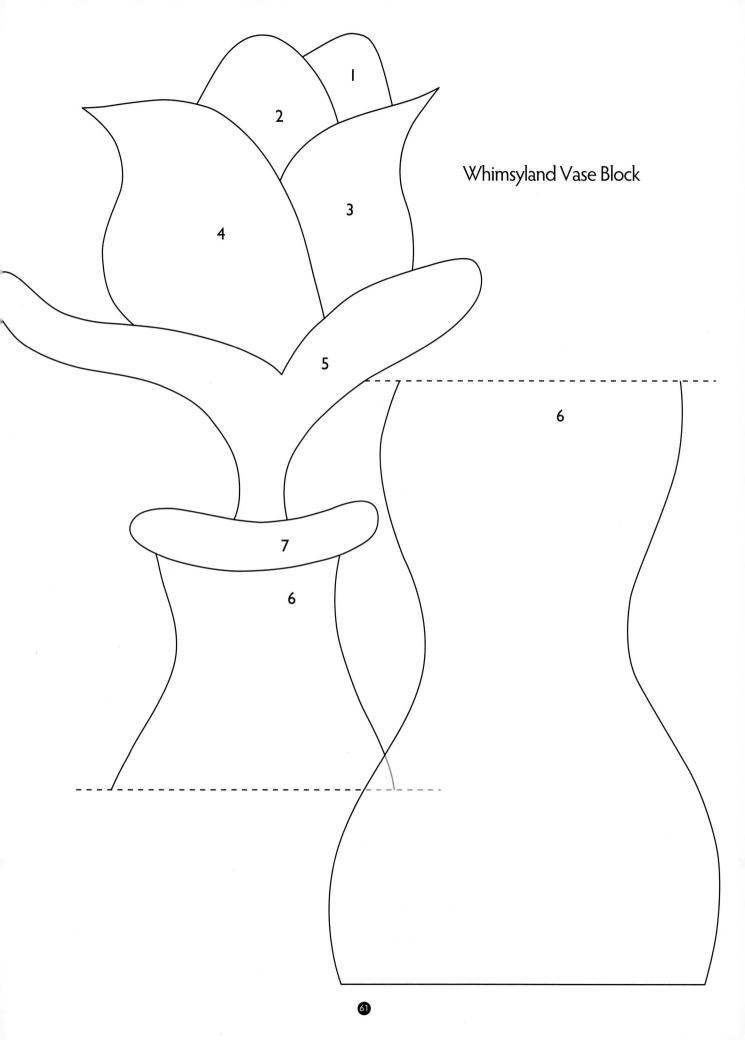

Whimsyland Vase Block

Whimsyland Cinnafleur Block
(single flower)

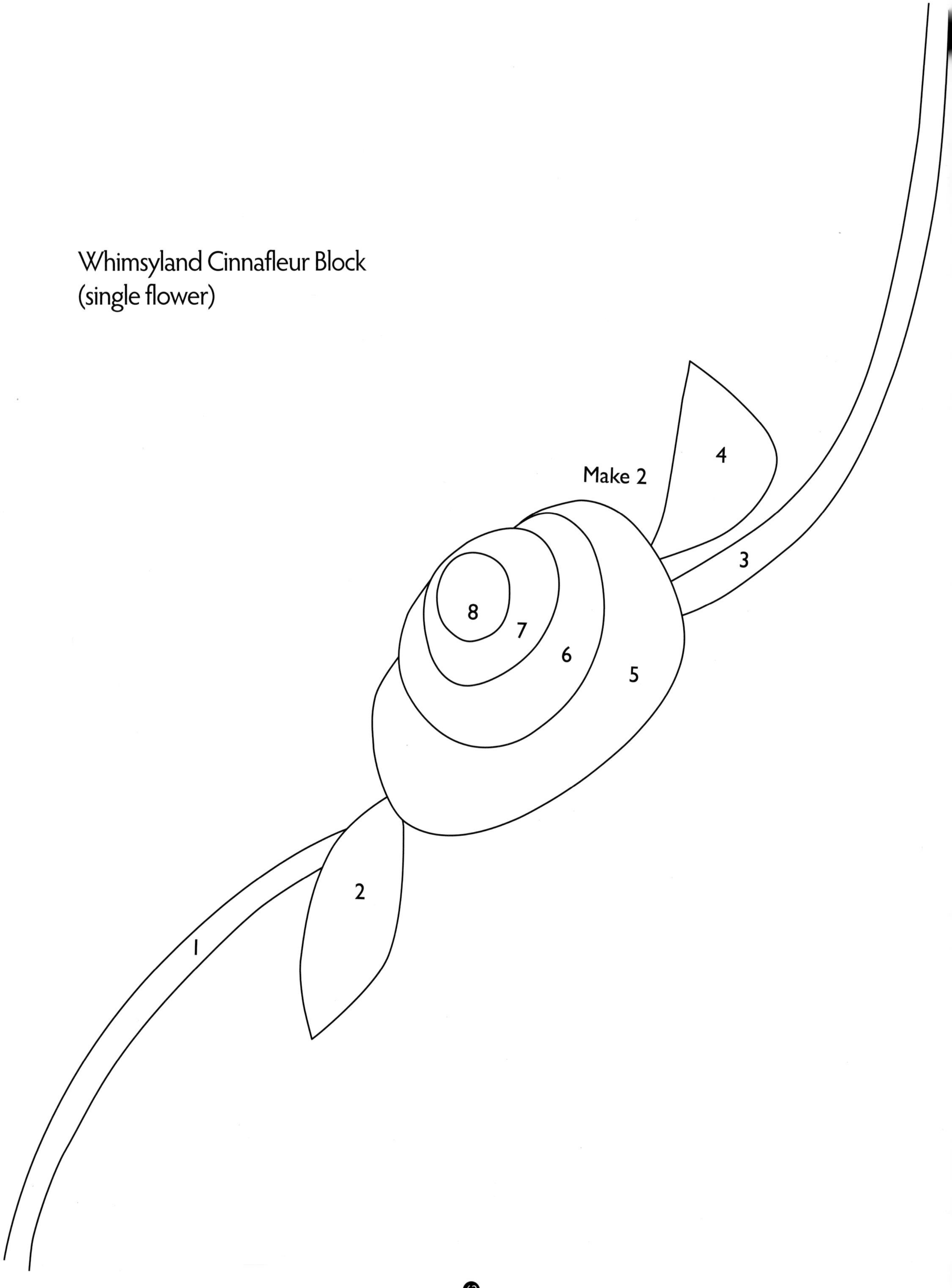

Make 2

4

3

8

7

6

5

2

1

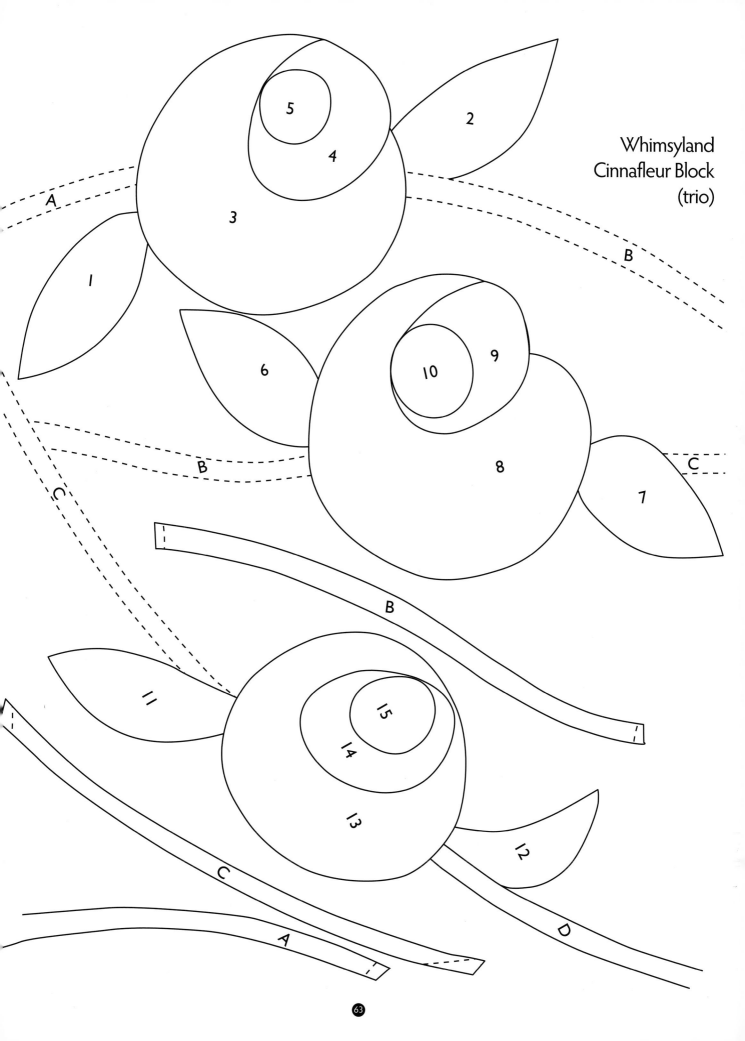

Whimsyland
Cinnafleur Block
(trio)

Whimsyland
Sunny Flower Block

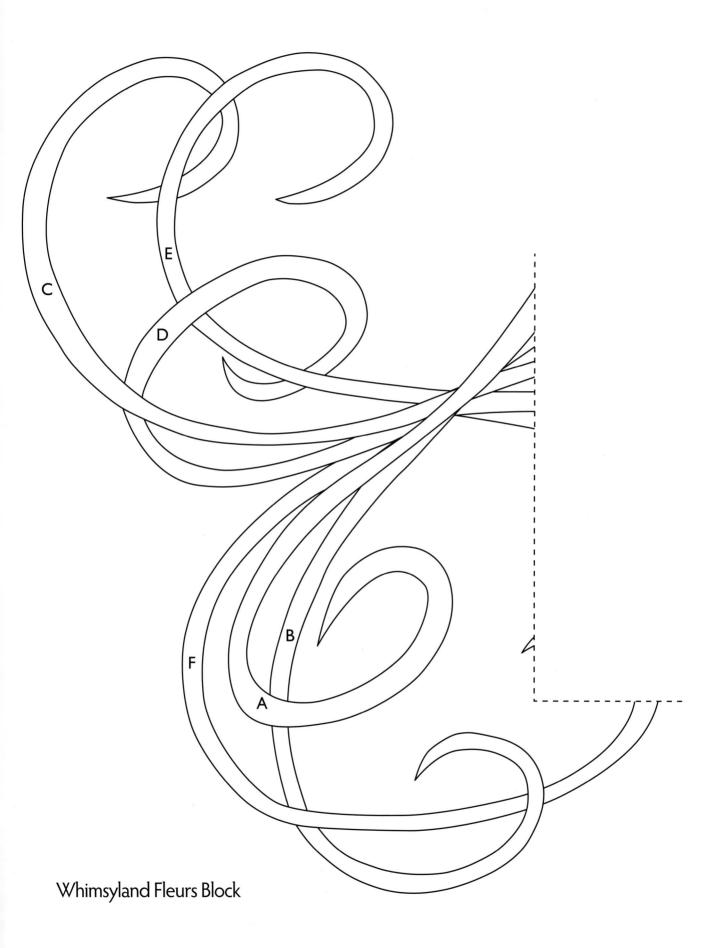

Whimsyland Fleurs Block

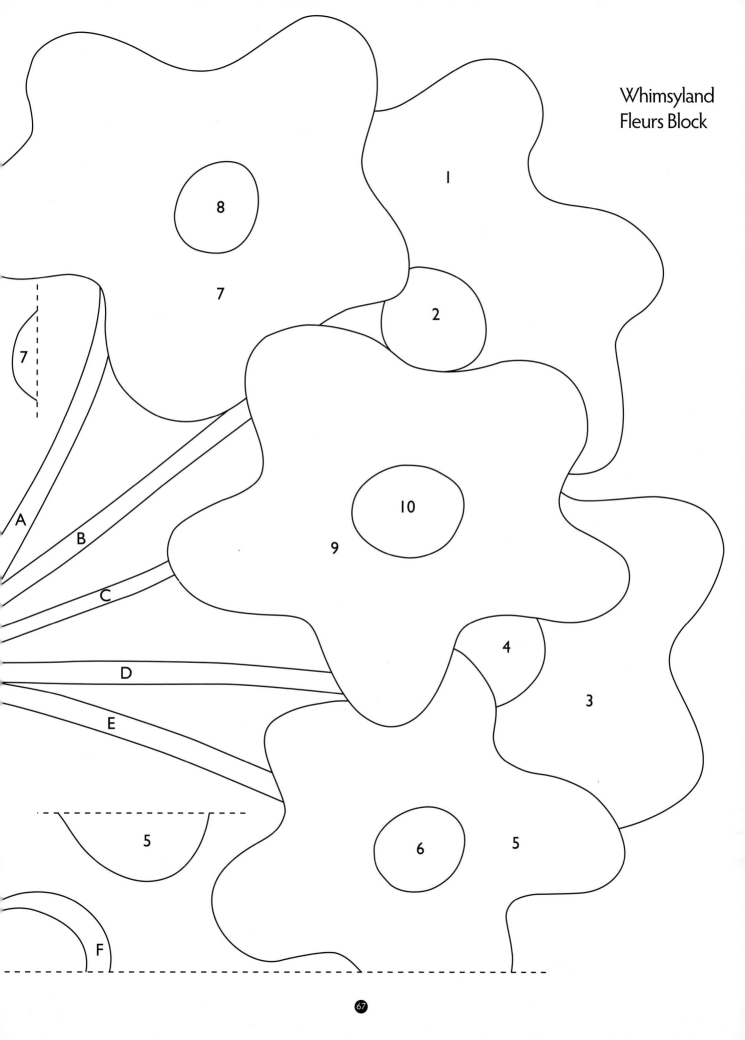

Whimsyland
Fleurs Block

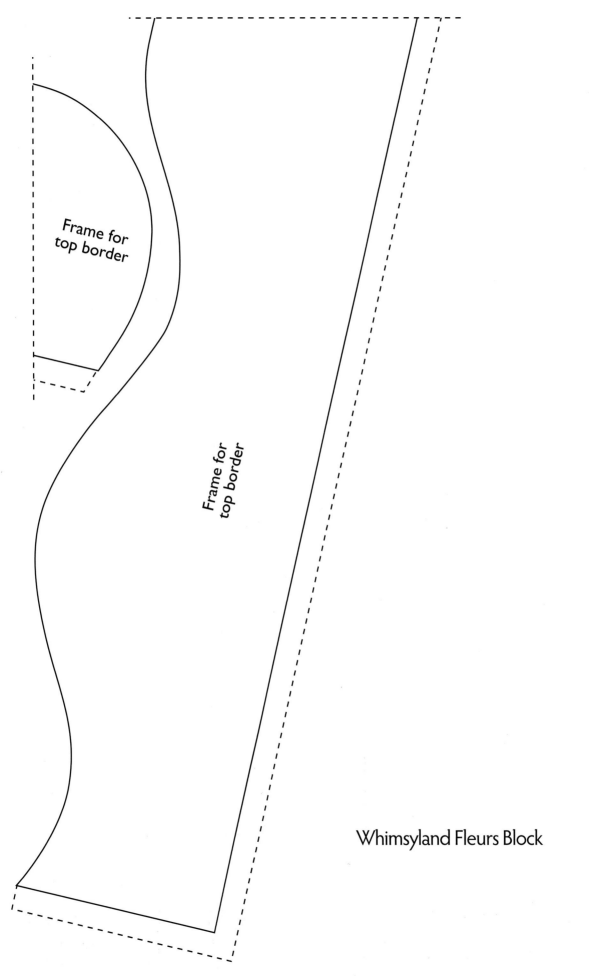

Frame for
top border

Frame for
top border

Whimsyland Fleurs Block

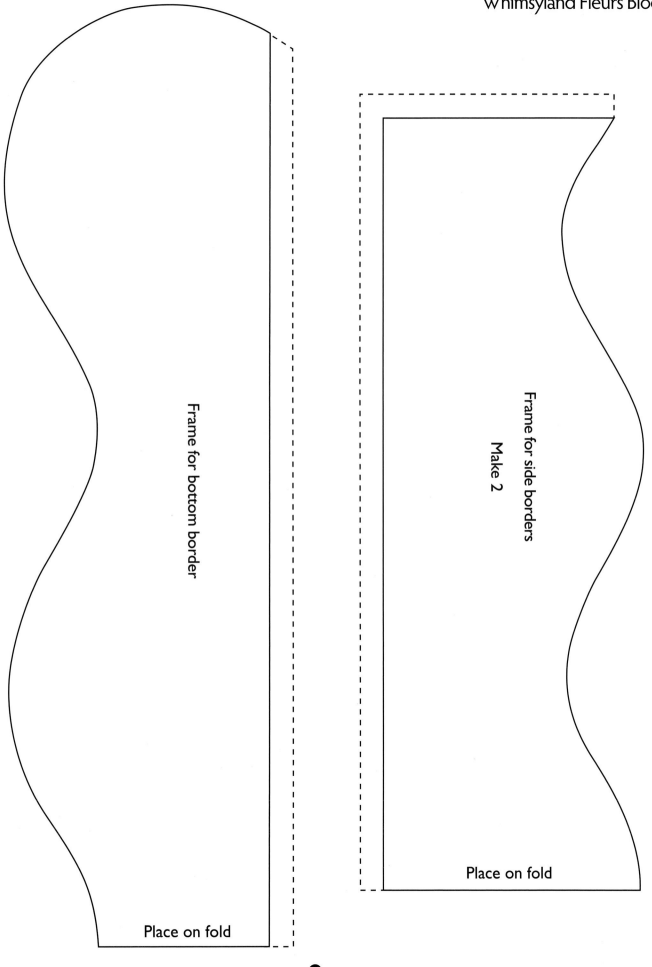

Frame for bottom border

Place on fold

Frame for side borders

Make 2

Place on fold

Place on fold

Whimsyland Smile Block

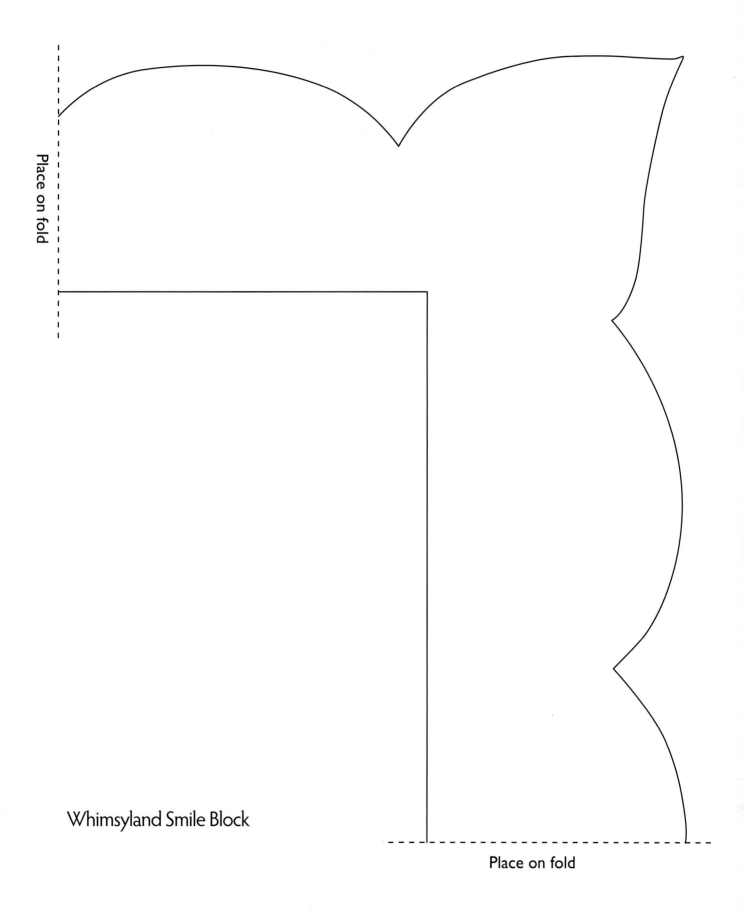

Place on fold

Whimsyland Smile Block

Place on fold

Whimsyland
House Block

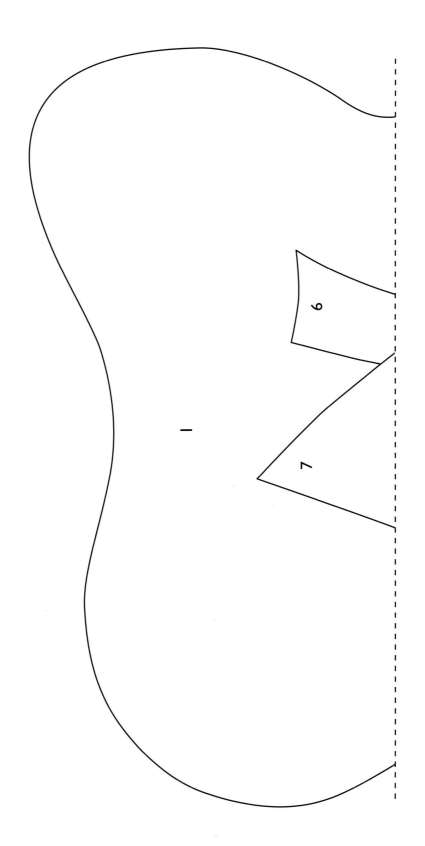

6

1

7

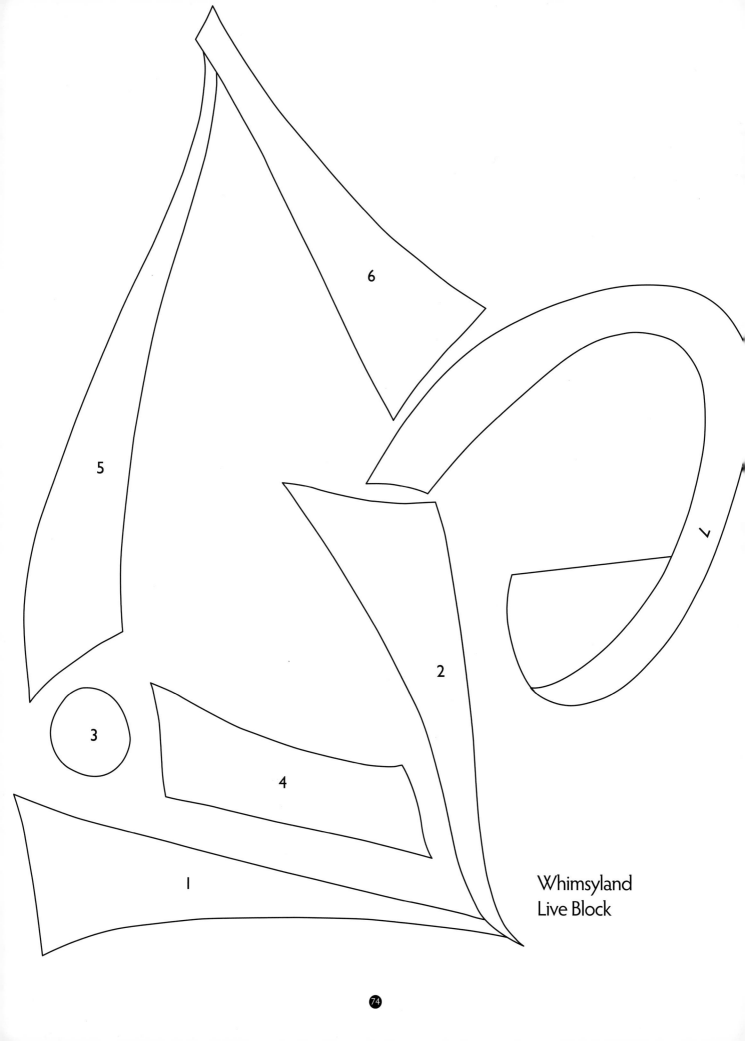

Whimsyland
Live Block

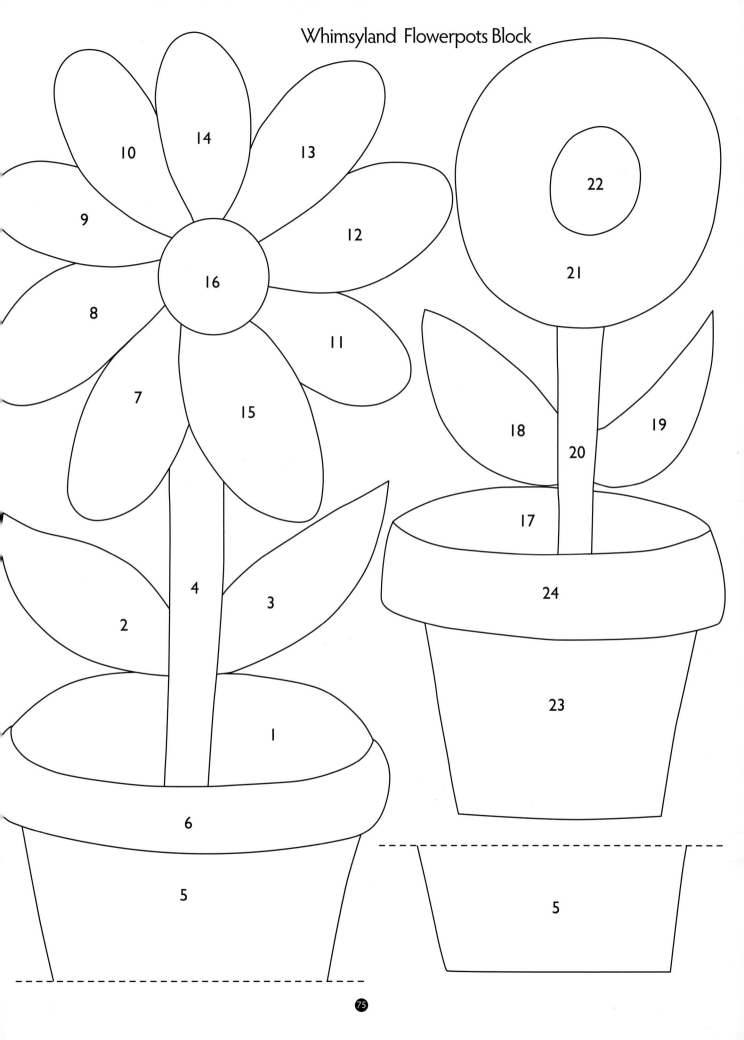

Whimsyland Flowerpots Block

75

Whimsyland
Funky Fleur Block

2

1

3

4

Whimsyland
Pieced Heart Block

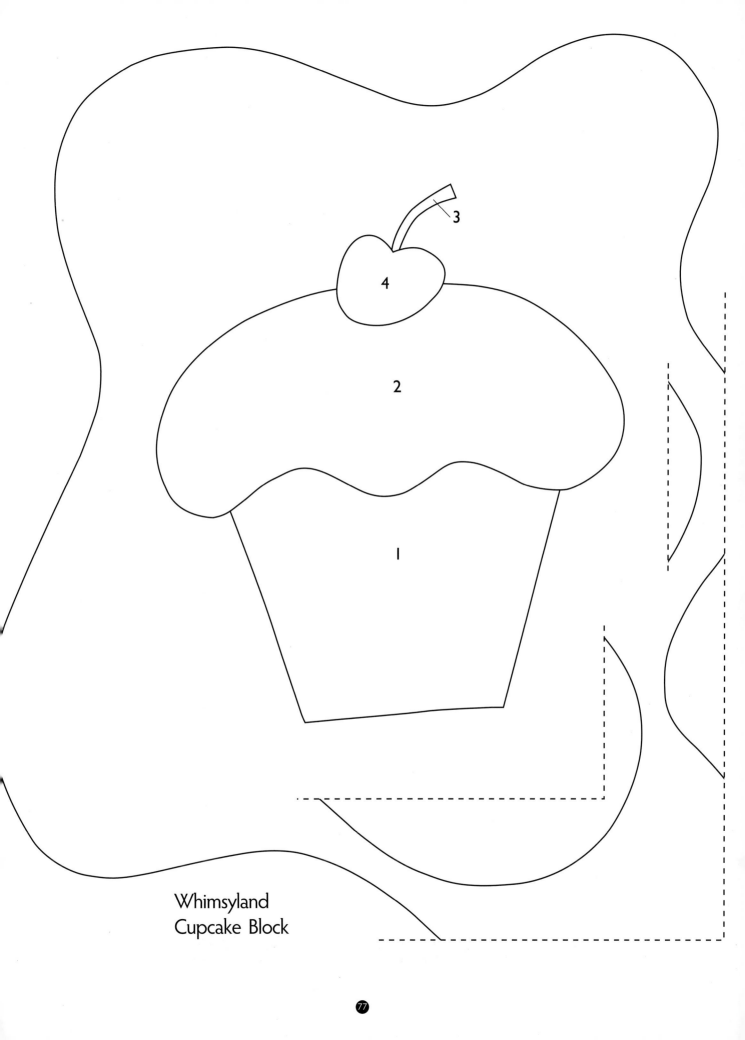

3

4

2

1

Whimsyland
Cupcake Block

Whimsyland
Dream Block

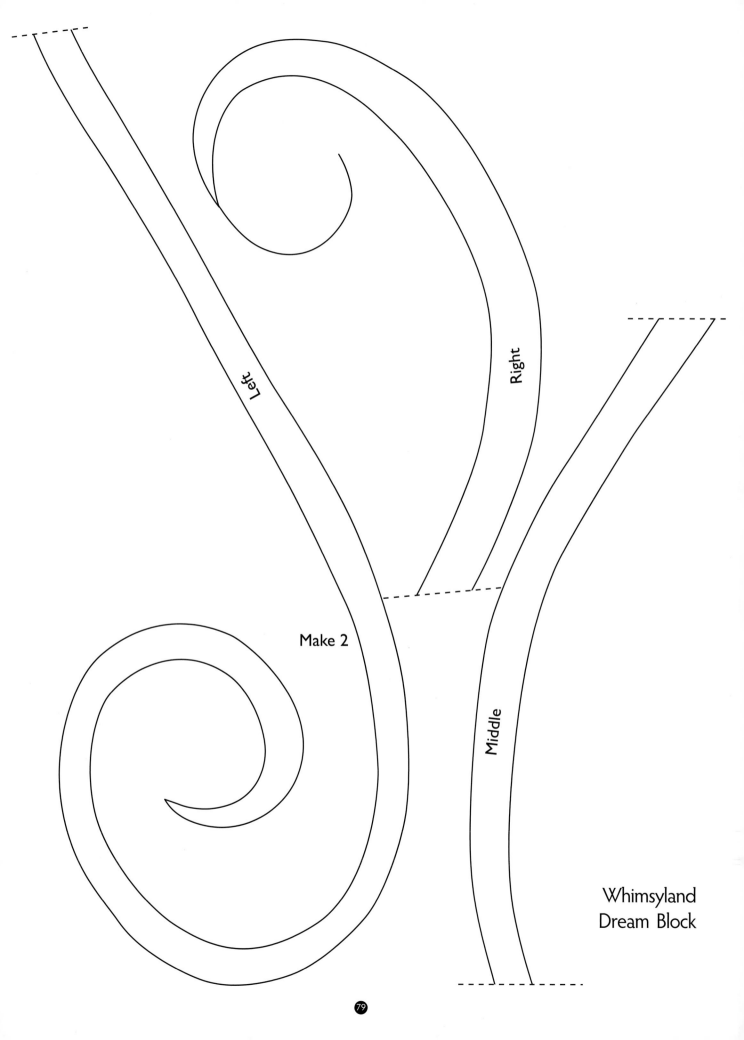

Left

Right

Make 2

Middle

Whimsyland
Dream Block

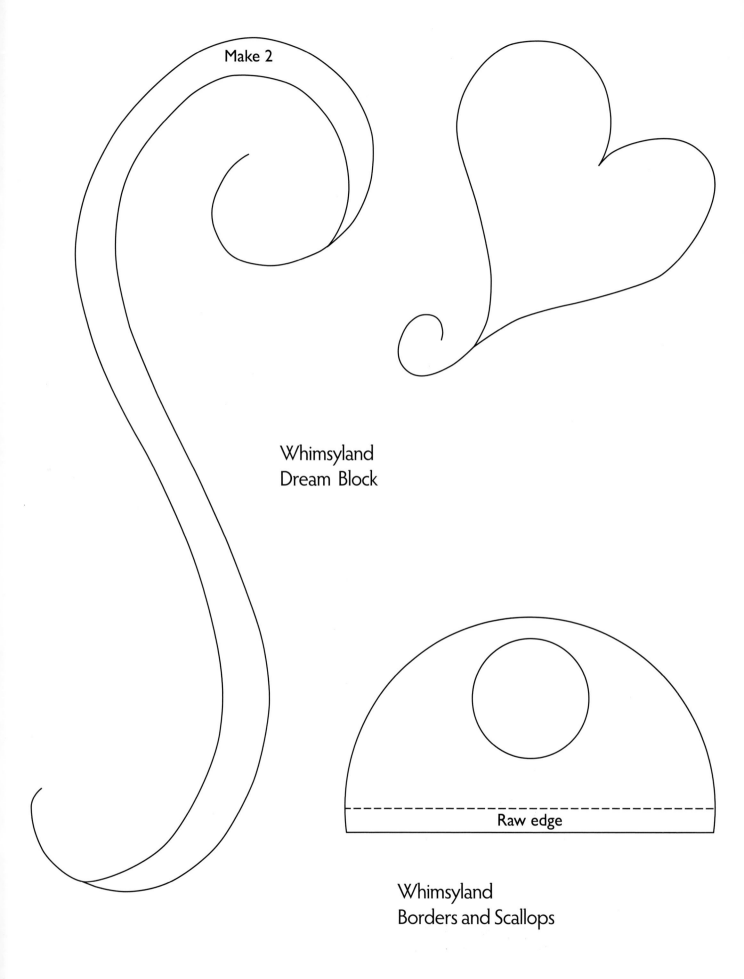

Make 2

Whimsyland
Dream Block

Raw edge

Whimsyland
Borders and Scallops

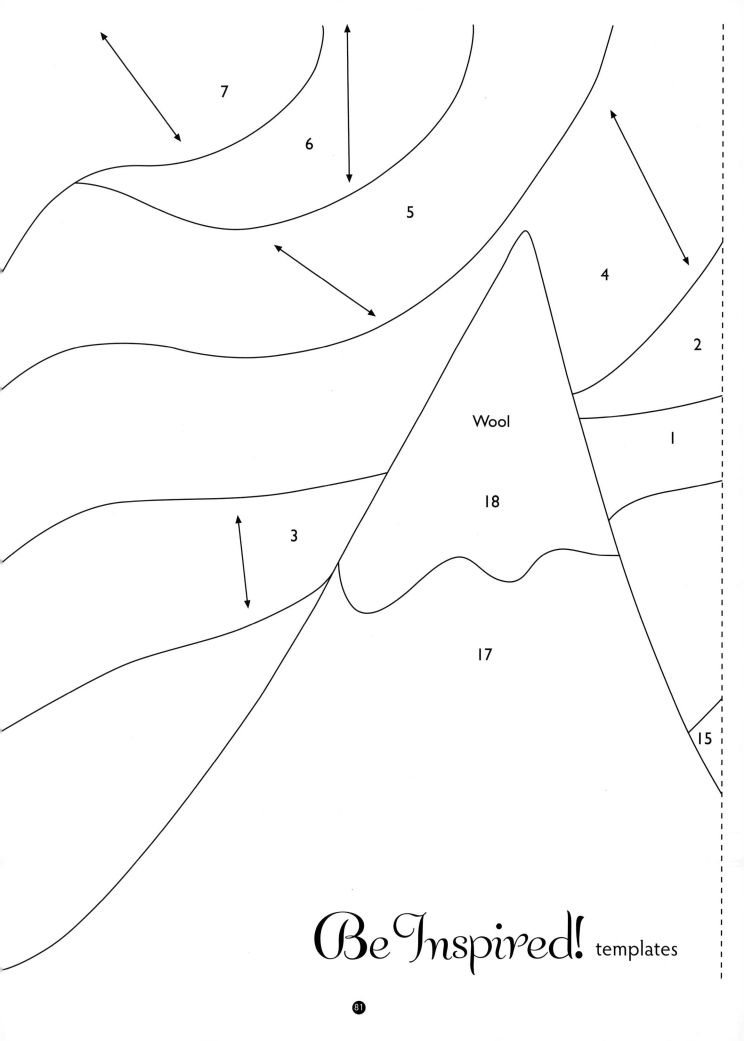

7

6

5

4

2

Wool

1

18

3

17

15

Be Inspired! templates

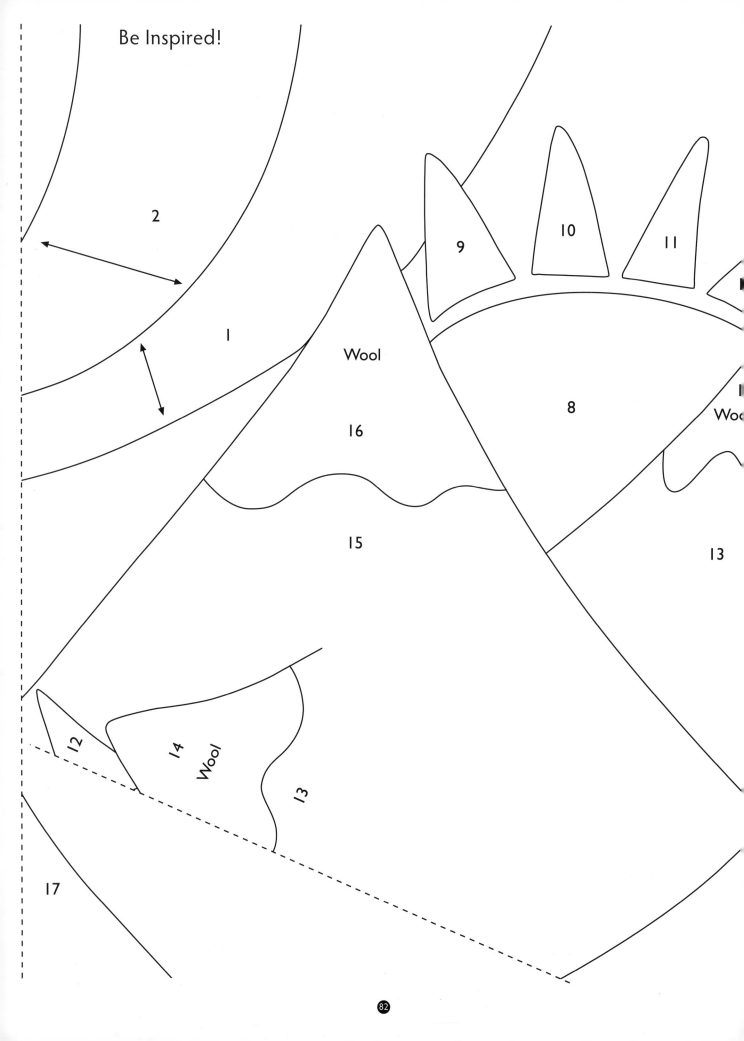

Be Inspired!

2

1

Wool

16

15

9

10

11

8

Wool

13

12

14
Wool

13

17

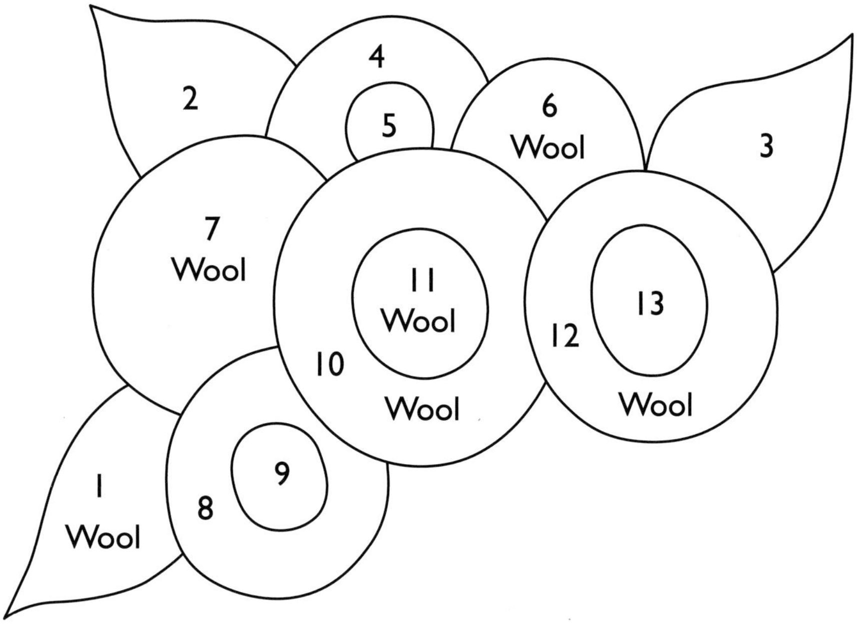

Be Inspired!

2

4

5

6
Wool

3

7
Wool

11
Wool

13

10

12

Wool

Wool

1
Wool

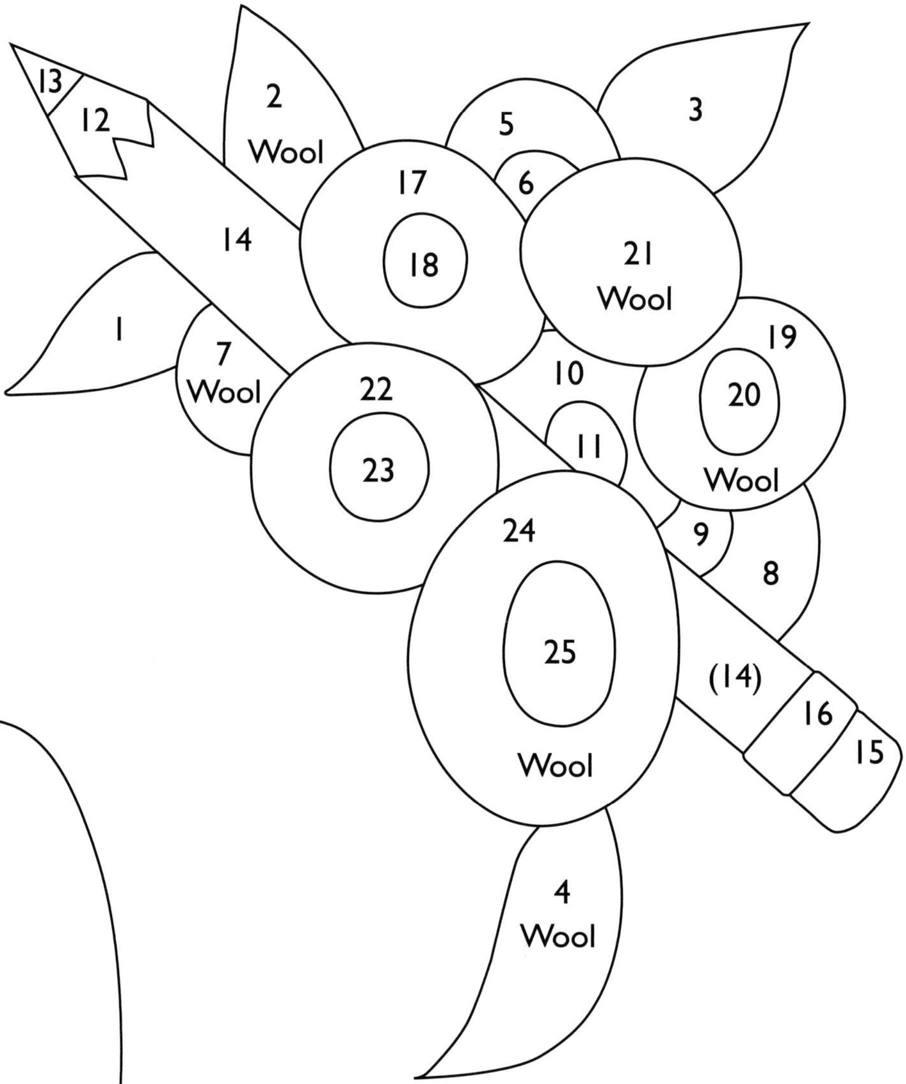

8

9

13

12

2
Wool

5

3

14

17

6

21
Wool

1

18

19

7
Wool

22

10

20
Wool

23

11

9

8

24

25

(14)

16

Wool

15

4
Wool

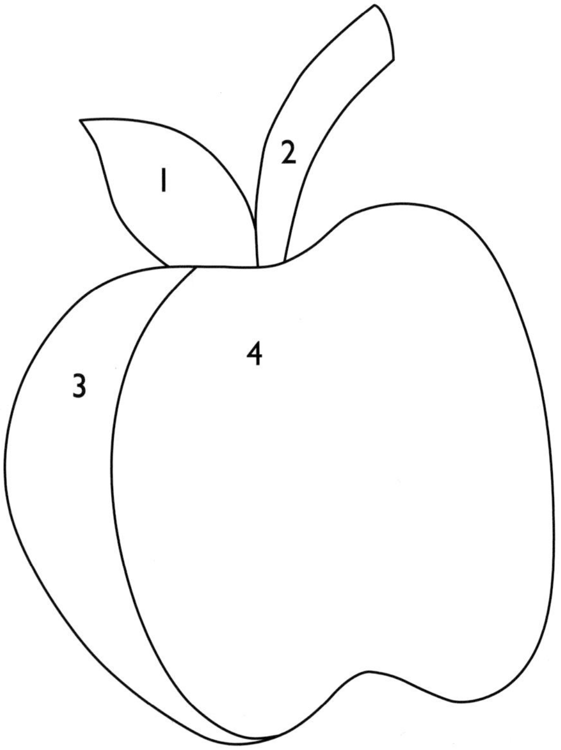

1

2

3

4

84

13

10   12   11

14

9

7

8

1

then teac

Be Inspired!

others

Live to learn to learn to live

The Lizzie-Bean Bag Chair

templates

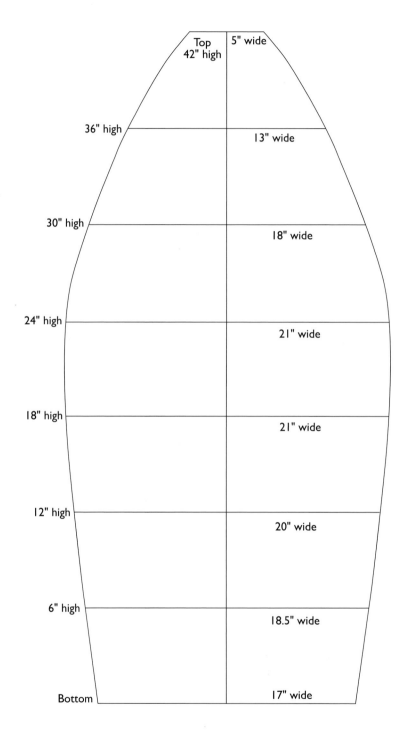

Top
42" high

5" wide

36" high

13" wide

30" high

18" wide

24" high

21" wide

18" high

21" wide

12" high

20" wide

6" high

18.5" wide

Bottom

17" wide

Beanbag Panel Dimensions:
Enlarge diagram 600% for a full-sized template,
or make your own using the dimensions shown.

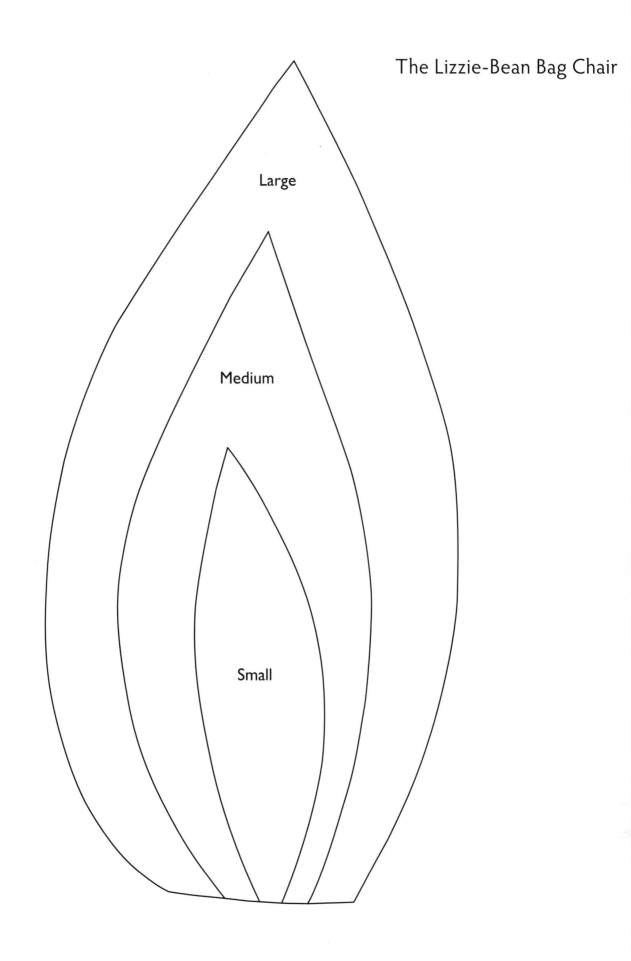

Large

Medium

Small

The Lizzie-Bean Bag Chair

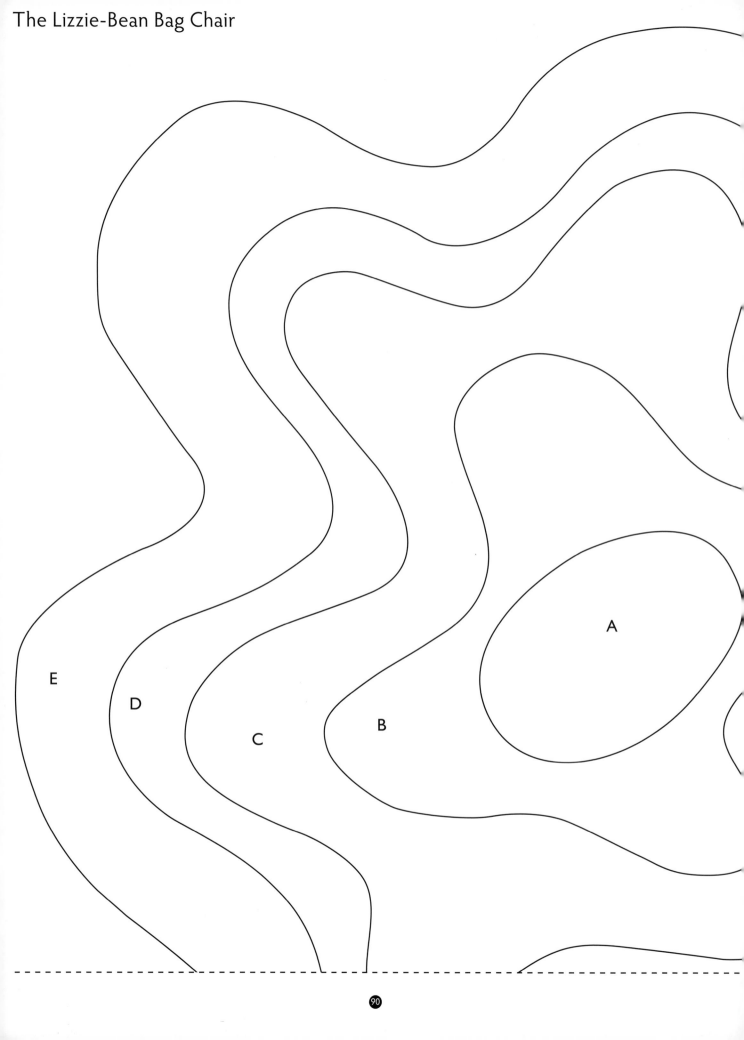

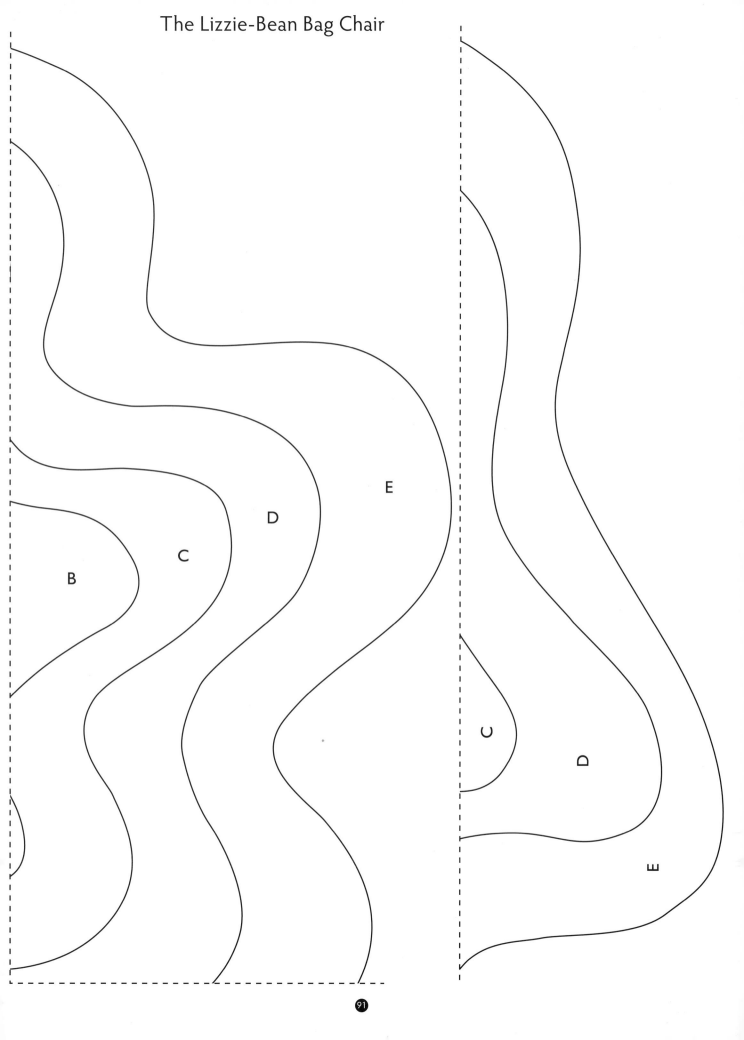

The Lizzie-Bean Bag Chair

B

C

D

E

C

D

E

91

Laugh A Good
Laugh templates

4

3

2

5

6

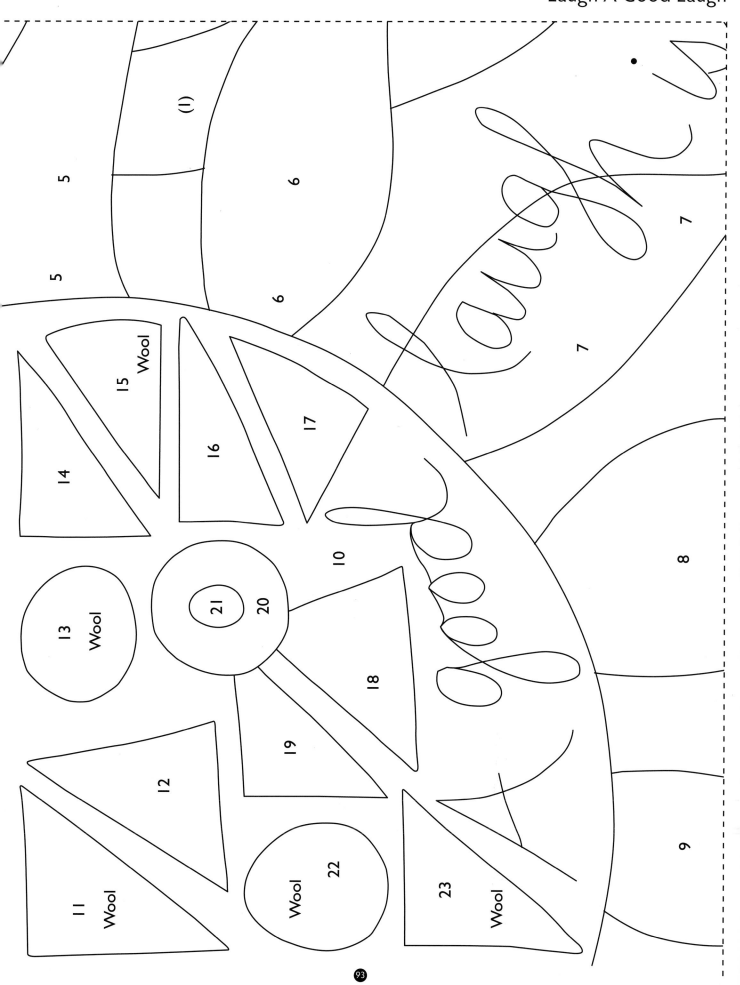

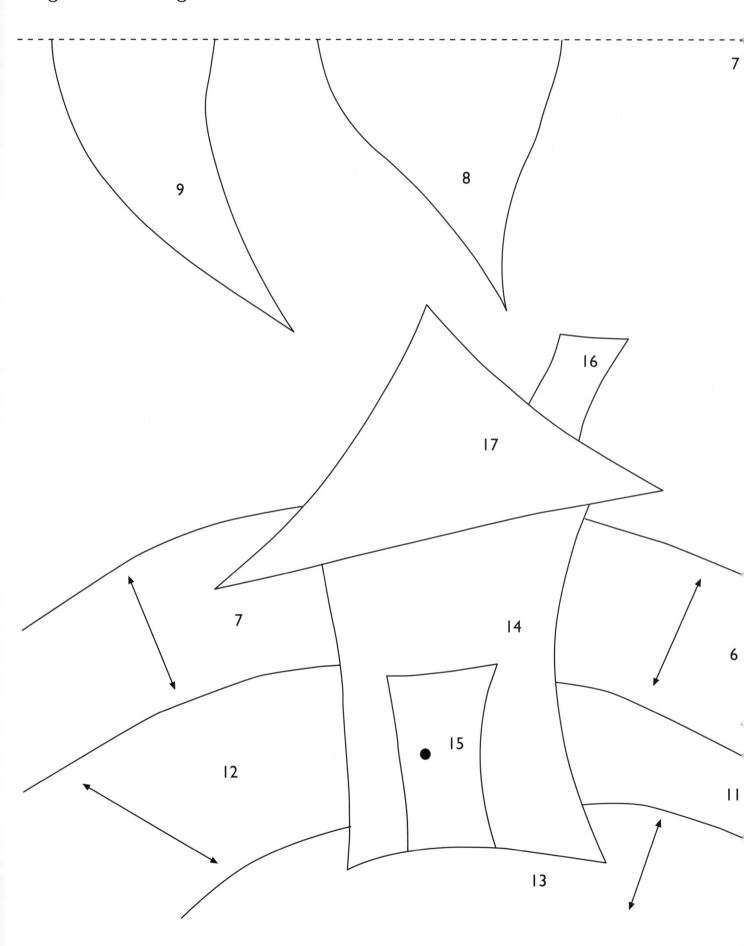

Laugh A Good Laugh

Laugh A Good Laugh

Laugh A Good Laugh

Fleur Rug templates

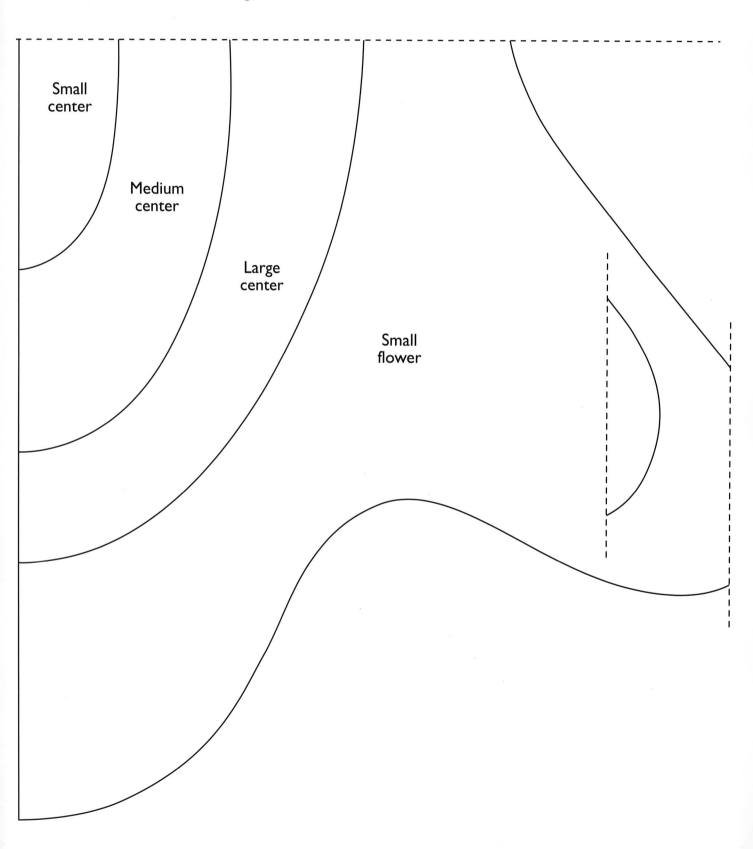

Small
center

Medium
center

Large
center

Small
flower

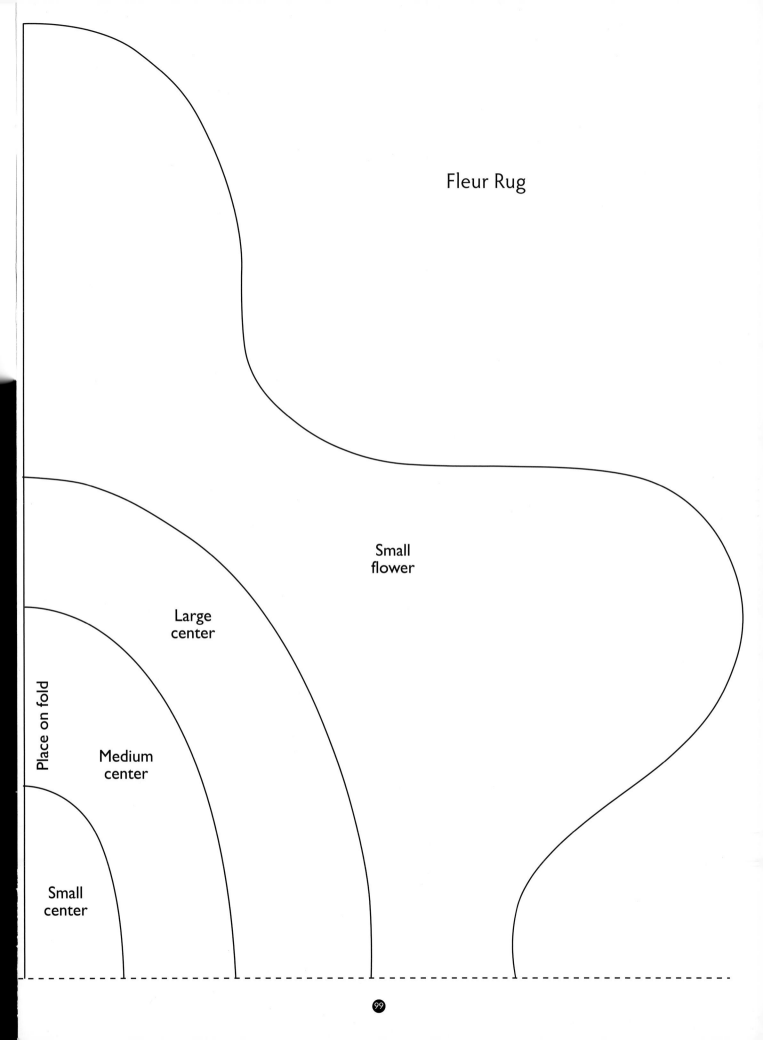

Fleur Rug

Small
flower

Large
center

Place on fold

Medium
center

Small
center

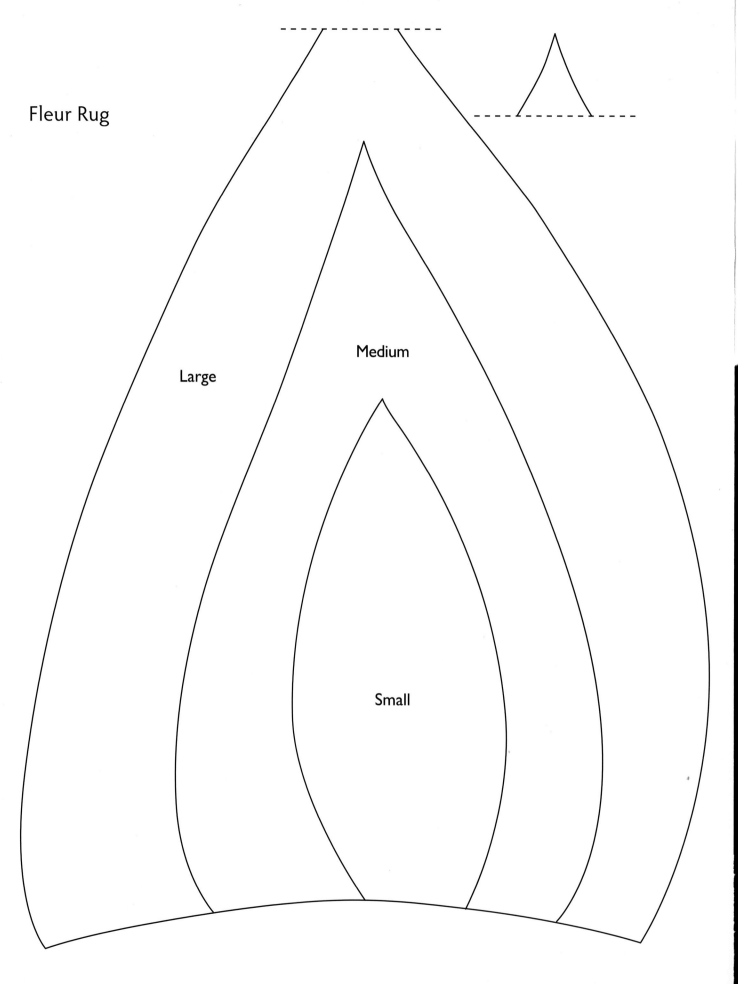

Fleur Rug

Large

Medium

Small

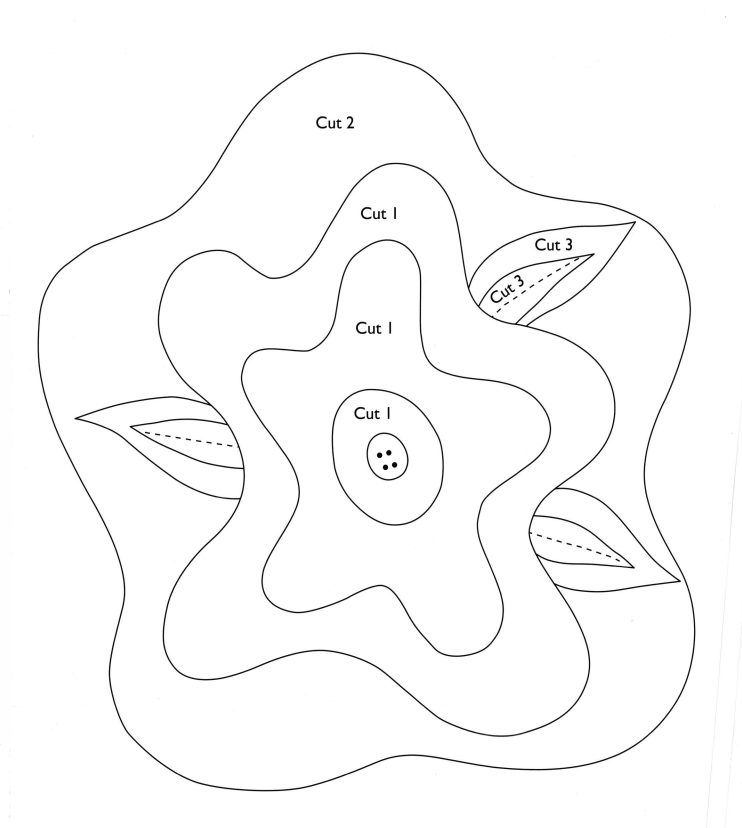

Cut 2

Cut 1

Cut 3

Cut 3

Cut 1

Cut 1

Cut 1

Cre8ive Dreamin'

A blast from the past

grew up in the middle of a large family and now realize that many of my childhood experiences somehow make their way into a quilt design. It's astounding what the subconscious mind hangs on to and throws back at you at any given moment! Not long after Lizzie B had hit the market and sales started taking off, I had a dream that reminded me just where our favorite flower design came from.

It was the "summer of the egg," as my siblings and I lovingly refer to it. In my family, I was number three out of six kids, and one summer my Mom announced that we'd all be in charge of our own breakfast and lunch. We were excited! Breakfast was no big deal, we knew how to pour cereal and milk. It was lunch that had us dreaming up new and exciting things to make. It was also in the early years of the microwave, kicking that creativity level up a notch! The question every day was: what can we make for lunch today in the microwave? The possibilities were endless. We microwaved just about anything. Some exploded. Most were inedible. But it was

The question every day was: what can we make for lunch today in the microwave? The possibilities were endless.

fun nonetheless! Pretty soon we got bored with nuking soup and sandwiches (even the peanut butter/marshmallow/chocolate chip ones!), so Mom told us to try cooking eggs.

Wow, eggs? That was big time! We all learned how to crack the eggs making sure no shells were left behind. Then started the egg cooking experiments. Scrambled eggs, runny eggs (sunny side up), eggs on toast (with or without the peanut butter!) you name it...we made it! But our very favorite? Poached eggs in the microwave. We are talking gourmet here. I'm not sure where the idea or "recipe" came from, but this was the '70s...not the prettiest decade. To poach our microwave eggs, we took a small custard cup, lined it with a nice round slice of bologna and cracked an egg right in the middle. Then we popped that baby into the microwave and watched that microwave magic cast its spell. In just a short minute or two, the egg cooked just like a poached egg and the bologna edges curled up so that by the time the timer beep, beep, beeped the finished delectable dish looked just like a...FLOWER!

Some thirty years later, the very same flower made a reappearance on one of the first Lizzie B quilts and people all over the world began stitching its lovely petals! We now refer to it as the Lizzie B Fleur...but know that really, it's a bologna flower. — *Liz Hawkins*

Liz at a young age sitting on her Daddy's lap, already dreamin' by the look on her face! Perhaps she gets her creative spark from Dad...notice his shirt and tie combo. Opposite: What do you get when you cross a creative childhood in the '70s with the dawning of the microwave? A scrumptious dish for any decade.

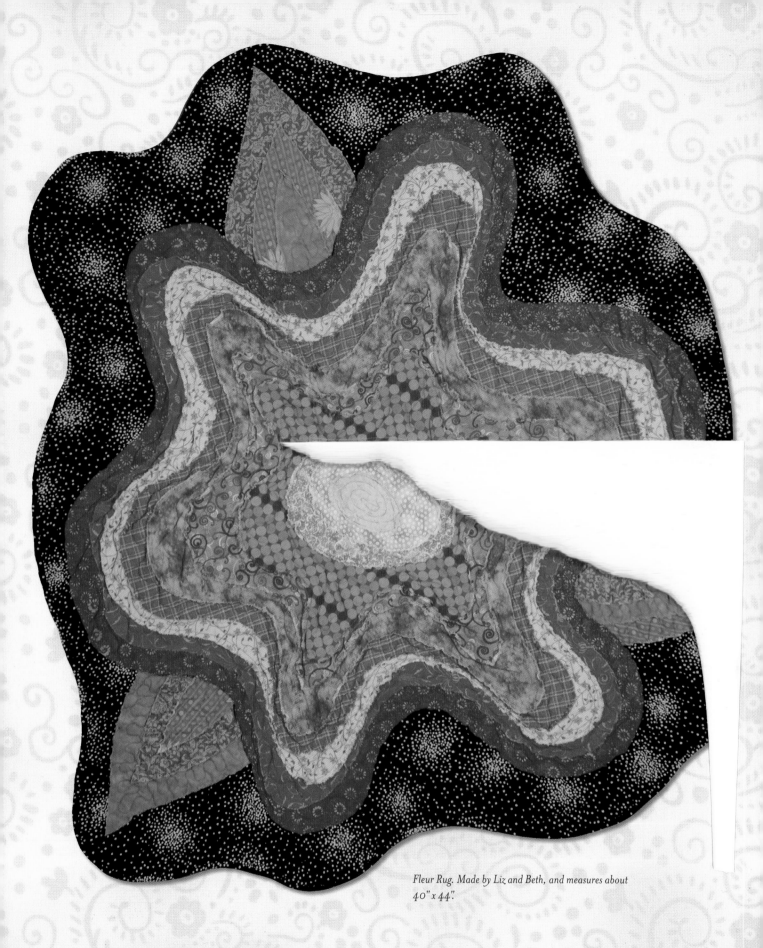

Fleur Rug. Made by Liz and Beth, and measures about 40" x 44".

Fleur Rug

Approx. 40" x 44"

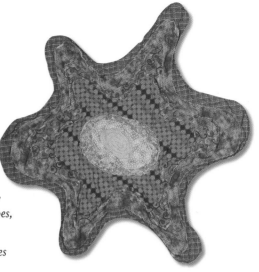

*Inspired by our good friend Gina Halladay...we took her quilted floor rug idea, and spun it around the Lizzie B studio! Using one of our whimsical flower shapes, and layering lots of fabrics both for weight and a splash of color...**voilà**...the Lizzie B "Fleur" rug was born! The fuzzy, raw edges are perfect for tired tootsies to sink into at the end of a day.*

CUTTING INSTRUCTIONS

❀ From the black fabric, cut a length of fabric 44" x width of fabric. Set aside the remainder of the black fabric to use for the binding.

❀ Use the template to make the small flower pattern. This flower should measure about 17" across. Make a pattern for each of the next 6 flower layers, by hand-drawing another flower about 1½" out from the edges of the previous flower shape. Each flower layer is about 3" larger in total than the one previous. The largest flower measures about 38" across.

❀ Cut the small flower shape from the orange fat quarter, and the 6 larger flower shapes from the pink fabrics.

❀ Cut a small, medium, and large flower center from the yellow fabrics.

❀ Cut a small, medium, and large leaf from each of the blue/green fabrics, for a total of 9 leaves.

SEWING INSTRUCTIONS

1. Make the leaves by mixing up the three fabrics. Layer a medium leaf on top of a large leaf, and machine stitch along the curved edges of the medium leaf, using a ¼" seam allowance. Place a small leaf on top, and stitch around the edge. Repeat for all three leaves.

2. Place the largest flower shape in the center of the black background square, and pin in place. Tuck the leaves in about ½" under the flower edge, and pin. Stitch the large leaves onto the background, using a ¼" seam allowance, and moving the flower out of the way as you stitch.

FABRIC REQUIREMENTS

- Black background and binding, 2 yards
- 6 pinks for flower: one pink 1 1/4 yards, four pinks 1 yard each, and one pink 3/4 yard
- 1 orange for flower, one fat quarter
- 3 yellows for center: one piece 4" x 5", one piece 6" x 8", and one piece 8" x 10"
- 3 blue/greens for leaves, one fat quarter of each
- Backing, 1 1/4 yards
- Cotton batting, crib-sized

Templates on pages 98-100

3. Stitch all around the flower shape, making sure to stitch over the base of the leaves.

4. Layer the next flower shape on top of the first, and stitch in place. Repeat for all the flowers.

5. Add the yellow centers to the flower, and stitch in place.

Fleur Rug continued

FINISHING

1. Use a white marking pencil or chalk marker to trace the outside edge of the rug onto the black fabric. Just draw curvy lines that somewhat mimic the edge of the flower, to give your rug a nice shape. Do **not** cut along the line quite yet!

2. Layer the rug top with the backing fabric and batting, just like a quilt. Machine quilt as desired, using the curvy edge line that you drew as a guide. You must be careful **not** to quilt over the flower raw edges, or your rug will not fluff as much when washed!

3. Cut the binding for the rug on the **bias**, so that the binding will curve around the rug edge. Sew the binding along the drawn curvy lines, just like a quilt! Then you may trim to the rug shape, and handstitch the other side of the binding down.

WASHING AND FLUFFING!

✿ After you have quilted and sewn the binding on your rug, you may fluff! The easiest way to do this is with a chenille brush, sold in quilt stores. Spritz a little water on the raw edges, a little back and forth with the brush…and the edges will fluff nicely. Once you have brushed all of the blocks, wash your rug **gently** in cold water and then tumble dry. You will need to trim a little of the longer threads, but then your rug will be ready to use!

What a fabulous way to hop outta bed each morning…Climb out from under your Topsy-Turvy Duvet Cover, and the first thing you'll see and feel is this cushy and colorful Fleur Rug!

The "Stick it to Me, Baby" pin cushion, about 8" diameter.
Stuck with cute Brighton push pins and stitched by Beth Hawkins.

Stick it to Me, Baby!

About 8" Diameter

*Tired of the same old "tomato" pincushion? (Which is never big enough to hold all your pins anyway!) This oversized flower adds a bit of whimsy to your sewing table. It's made of fabulous wool and is big enough to hold all your pins **and** your neighbor's pins too! Ah heck, forget the pins... scatter these in all sizes around your house! How **cute** are they anyway? Stick a wire in there and add a photo...or use it as a recipe holder...or a paperweight...etc. See where we're goin' here?*

CUTTING INSTRUCTIONS

❀ Use the template to cut 1 large flower, 1 small flower, 1 center, 3 large leaves, and 3 small leaves from the wool pieces. Do not add an additional seam allowance to the wool pieces.

❀ Cut out just **ONE** pincushion shape from the black wool. Add ¼" seam allowance to the template. Do not cut the other shape yet, just leave the remainder of the black wool intact.

SEWING INSTRUCTIONS

1. Layer a small leaf on top of a large leaf, and machine stitch down the center of both layers. Repeat for all three leaves.

2. Place the flower shapes onto the cutout pincushion shape, and pin in place. Tuck the leaves in about ¾" under the flowers.

3. Stitch around the flower shapes only, a scant ¼" in from the edge of the wool. The leaves are left loose, but make sure they are secured by the flower stitching.

4. Place the top of the pincushion on the remaining piece of black wool, flower side down. Pin around all the edges. Make sure the leaves will not get caught as you stitch the edge.

5. Stitch around the top pincushion shape. Leave a 3" opening for turning and stuffing.

6. Trim the bottom black wool piece to match the top. Turn right side out.

SUPPLY LIST

- Black wool, 9" x 18"
- Wool for flower, one 6" x 7" piece, one 4" x 5" piece, and one 2" square for the center
- Green for leaves, one 3" x 5" piece, and one 2" x 3" piece
- Buttons for center, one yellow and one black
- Filling for pincushion (We used finely crushed walnut shells, from the pet store!)

Templates on page 101

7. Use a small funnel to stuff the pincushion with the walnut shells. You could also use poly-fil stuffing if you wish. Stuff it tightly, making sure all the curves are filled out. Use a scrap piece of wool or poly-fil to "seal" the opening, so that the filling does not spill out when you hand-stitch the opening closed.

8. Using a very long darning needle, and a double-strand of Perle Cotton, attach a yellow button to the center of the flower, and at the same time, a small black button to the bottom center for added strength. Pull it tightly as you stitch, causing an indentation in the center of the pincushion. Tie it off at the bottom with a really good knot!